D0882988

POETS NOW

Edited by Robert Peters

1. *Jonathan Williams*, Get Hot or Get Out
2. *Rochelle Ratner*, Practicing To Be A Woman
3. *Jerry Ratch*, Hot Weather
4. *David Ray*, The Touched Life
5. *Carolyn Stoloff*, A Spool of Blue
6. *Edwin Honig*, Interrupted Praise

For Billy Collins —
with Admiration —
David Ray
X-mas 2001

THE TOUCHED LIFE

Poems

Selected and New
by David Ray

David Ray

Poets Now 4

The Scarecrow Press, Inc.
Metuchen, N.J., & London 1982

BOOKS BY DAVID RAY

Poetry

X-RAYS, Cornell University Press, 1965
DRAGGING THE MAIN, Cornell University Press, 1968
A HILL IN OKLAHOMA, BkMk Press, 1972
GATHERING FIREWOOD, Wesleyan University Press, 1974
ENOUGH OF FLYING, Writers Workshop (Calcutta, India), 1977
THE TRAMP'S CUP, Chariton Review Press, 1978
ORPHANS, The Pancake Press, 1981

Fiction

THE MULBERRIES OF MINGO, Cold Mountain Press, 1978

Audiocassettes

AN OLD NICKEL & DIME STORE, Watershed Foundation
THE TRAMP'S CUP, New Letters on the Air
ENOUGH OF FLYING, New Letters on the Air

Library of Congress Cataloging in Publication Data

Ray, David, 1932-
   The touched life.

   (Poets now ; 4)
   I. Title.   II. Series.
PS3568.A9T6   811'.54   82-3371
ISBN 0-8108-1535-4   AACR2

Copyright © 1982 by David Ray
Manufactured in the United States of America

INTRODUCTION

Since 1965, when his X-Rays appeared, David Ray has published seven books of poetry and The Mulberries of Mingo and Other Stories. He has also edited numerous anthologies and, since 1971, New Letters, an influential little magazine. This present volume contains substantial portions of his published poetry, plus a generous selection of work appearing in book form for the first time.

The poem "Mulberries" documents a tormented childhood. A boy and his sister are locked out of the family house, because of the mother's indifference and the father's cruelty. When they are hungry all they have to eat is mulberry fruit. Now, as a grown man, Ray is brushing fallen fruit into a pile, to "nourish" his linden and birch trees. The mulberries, he declares, are "good for nothing but to make us / slip and break our bones." He shifts to a sudden defiance: "I never want my children/to eat mulberries." Why? Because he and his sister had taken them "into their bellies / with defeat." This poem sounds so simple! And when Ray spins that final line the impact is like a kick in the gut.

Many other poems have a similar power. "Orphans," one of the longest, is also about brutalizing children. The sadistic matrons

> . . . enjoy hurling the miserable child
> down stairs, hearing him weep in the night,

enjoy making him eat turnips or whatever
makes him throw up, enjoy cutting the blonde
girl's braids, throwing them into the toilet,
reminding her that no mother wants a lock
of that hair to save. They enjoy pinching
the small buttons of the girl's nipples . . .

These were the abandoned children "of living drunks," of
mothers who disappeared with truckdrivers, or of parents
who "locked their children out to eat mulberries / in the
churchyard tree." Such a life teaches a gritty survival; and
"like rats in alleys" these youngsters survive:

as only the children of true spirits can,
whose mothers are stars,
whose fathers are ash,
whose cousins are the pebbles around rose
bushes which would not even tear
the nylons of false mothers as they fled us.

"Chiggers" is also about childhood anxieties. A teenage
uncle frightens the child by telling him that when three
chiggers manage to bore straight through his body he will
die. As Ray follows his father down freshly plowed furrows,
he sees three red dots on his belly. Later, when he bathes in
the smokehouse tub, uses potash soap, and steams "under
the hams of hogs" he'd known by name, he believes he will
continue to live.

Several poems seem devoted to exorcising a cruel,
neglectful father. In "Words at Midnight," one of the best of

Ray's poems, the exorcism seems to work. The opening echoes some of Robert Frost's cadences, as well as some of Frost's uncanny affection for the commonplace event — here it's getting a haircut:

> How often when some barber's put a dirty towel
> against my head and his thumb's caressed my neck
> with some sense of how tired and hopeless
> my life has been . . . .

Ray remembers a haircut he had in Mexico, on the eve of Mexican Independence Day. In a vision he sees his father, who had "shuffled out" most of his life "around a barber chair." The son felt maimed and trapped by the father, and although Ray has "never been a man for fireworks," he vows that if he ever gains his freedom from his father ("from you and your ever-present / absence") he'll "yell and throw fire everywhere." The father always had affection for his customers, but never for his son. The poem concludes with this simply and beautifully rendered insight; Ray seems to have made peace with his dad's memory:

> A life's a life
> so long as hope for change can send us
> running for a haircut to the Alameda fireworks.
> This you somehow know, and so, Dear Dad, do I.

Recalling Robert Frost helps us to see an important influence on Ray's style and attitudes. His "Thanks, Robert Frost," from *Orphans*, evokes the older poet's cadences and his hardy, no-nonsense views of life — an experiential wisdom as crabbed as a tart apple. The aged Frost is asked if he has "hope for the future":

> Yes, and even for the past, he replied,
> *that it will turn out to have been all right*
> *for what it was,* something we can accept,
> mistakes made by the selves we had to be,
> not able to be, perhaps, what we wished,
> or what looking back half the time it seems
> we could so easily have been, or ought . . . .

Ray moves then into his own brief Frostian meditation. Like Frost, he hopes that he can "bear" the future, as he must continue to bear the past. He apologizes to his children, for "those albatrosses" he has placed around their necks. Yes, he tells Frost, "your words provide that courage / and it brings strange peace that itself passes / into past, easier to bear because / you said it, rather casually, as snow / went on falling in Vermont years ago." In this poem to Frost, Ray's childhood and manhood merge.

"On the Photograph 'Yarn Mill,' by Lewis W. Hine" occasions Ray's reflections on his son, as the boy, Sam, stands near spinning machines ready to weave out his own life. Like the boy in the old photograph, Sam, trusting, "gazes almost amused / at what's before him." Boss men tell the boy what to do:

> the humming
> strings look like the innards

of long pianos whose music dins;
the yarn is beaten now by wooden
mallets, then woven — sheared,
combed, dyed — whatever
the boss men say, in North Carolina,
1908

In the 1970s, the orders remain, and the son must guard his
integrity against the powerful thrusts of overseers.

"At the Washing of My Son" commemorates Sam's
birth. This is Ray's record of his first glimpse of the newborn
boy:

You were still wrinkled, and had a hidden face,
Like a hedgehog or a mouse, and you crouched in
The black elbows of a Negro nurse. You were
Covered with your mother's blood, and I saw
That navel where you and I were joined to her . . . .

Many of Ray's poems move me; and many are quite
different from those I have been describing. Readers will
find their own favorites. "Throwing the Racetrack Cats at
Saratoga" exploits a bit of bizarre Americana. "Ribcage
Behind a Meat Counter" meditates on the carcass of a steer.
In "The Telephone" various dead persons talk to Ray. "For
the Stepfather" eulogizes old Lee, who rests in his grave
beneath a rusting anvil, symbol of his trade. Ray remem-
bers the old man's attempt to rape his sister. "Lunch in the
Cafeteria" occurs in a cancer ward.

Finally, what I have tried to show in this too-brief

introduction is that Ray is a brutally honest man; he sees life, in a sense, without eyelids. Though he has few illusions, he emerges as a vigorous celebrant of life. The critically examined life, he knows — good Emersonian that he is — is indeed worth living. His lyric style is supple and unostentatious. While reading him we share his "snapshots," a word he himself favors. His poems are human-centered, as snapshots are — records of intimate experience. And when he displays his album he does not bore us with mindless chatter. His observations, never otiose, are direct and moving. In his layering of snapshots of time he finds the hope that his mentor Robert Frost spoke of. Ray is a fresh and very American voice.

Robert Peters
Editor, *Poets Now*

CONTENTS

1. X·Rays

Greens 3
Two Farm Scenes 4
X-Ray 5
Midnight 6
The Card-Players 7
On a Fifteenth-Century Flemish Angel 7
A View of the Valley During Your Absence 8
On Reading That Napoleon Was Poisoned 9
Fourth of July 11
Chiggers 11
We Waited While the Landlady's Son 13
Deathlace 14
Redburn's Vertigo Compared 16
This Life 17

2. Dragging the Main

Coming into Portland 21
An Egyptian Couple in the Louvre 21
The Paseo in Irun 22
At the Train Station in Pamplona 23
Some Notes on Vietnam 24
The Way with Dissent 26

Lunch in the Cafeteria   27
Committee   29
The Waves   30
Thoughts of Malcolm Lowry   31
On Seeing a Movie Based on an Episode from
   President Kennedy's Life   32
The Family in the Hills   35
The Art Museum   35
The Mid-Evening Angst   36
My Daughter as a Nuisance   37
Doing Without   38
Having Too Much   39
Dragging the Main   40
At the Washing of My Son   43
The Steward   44

3. Gathering Firewood

Chekhov   49
A Hill in Oklahoma   50
Ravenna   52
Archeology   52
A Ruined Shack in the Hills   53
Nowata   53
The Touched Life   54
After Sappho   56
The Family   56

At the Spring 57
Note 57
Stopping near Highway 80 58
The Indians near Red Lake 59
An Old Five-and-Ten-Cent Store 61
Season's Greetings 62
Skid Row 63
Analysis 63
A Midnight Diner by Edward Hopper 64
Movements 66
W. C. W. 67
My Poems 67
The Archaic 68
In Greece 69
With Samuel 70
At Delos 70
Through Museum Glass 71
Discovering Old Hotels 71
The New Widow 72
Ada 73
In Heraklion 74
The Blue Duck 75
Judy, a Face 76
Gathering Firewood 78

4. Enough of Flying: Poems Inspired by the Ghazals of Ghalib   81

Confessions of a Happy Man   88

5. The Tramp's Cup

The Monastery in Scotland   93
Cousin Eric   95
The Greatest Poem in the World   95
A Dance on the Greek Island   97
Old Postcards   98
Words at Midnight   99
Missouri Wedding   100
Understanding Poetry   104
To One Who in His Love of Liberty   105
"Take Me Back to Tulsa"   108
Poe's Anvil   109
Snapshots   110
Scene in Calabria   111
A Swedish Postcard   112
Vincent   114
Hammering   116
Mummies & Others   118
Genitori   119
Marriage   120
The Interview   121
The Tramp's Cup   122

6. Orphans

Mulberries	127
Orphans	128
Envoi	133
Hymn to Aunt Edris	134
A Memory of West Tulsa and Long Beach	136
In the Gallery Room	137
On the Photograph "Yarn Mill," by Lewis W. Hine	138
Garage Sale	139
The Father	141
The Theme of Missed Opportunities	142
In Tornado Country	143
Thanks, Robert Frost	144
The Matter of Social Life	145
Sonnet to Seabrook	146
The Cenote at Chichen Itza	147
Three from Greece	148
Baskin's Wooden Angel	150
The Farm in Calabria	151

7. New Poems

Villanelle: Their Arrival	159
A Portrait of the Mexican Barber	160
The Wise Guys	161
Travelling and Sitting Still	162
The Tourist	163

Kitty Returns to Auschwitz 164
On the Island 166
To Queen Elizabeth 168
Throwing the Racetrack Cats at Saratoga 169
The Snake People 171
The Cigarette Factory 172
Tennessee 174
Migrant Mother, 1936 177
Marks on a Wall 178
Staying Over with Aunt Ruth 180
For the Stepfather 182
Another Garage Sale 183
The Old Man with the Shopping Cart 185
The Eskimo Girl 188
Another Assassin: Negative Capability 190
Ribcage Behind a Meat Counter 192
Saint Flannery 193
The Telephone 193
Getting to Know You 195
De Mortuis 197

X-RAYS

GREENS

A boy stoops, picking greens with his mother —
This is the scene in the great elm-shadows.
A pail stands by her feet, her dress conceals
Her chill knees, made bitter by the tall man
Who now lifts a glass, she thinks, with his friends,
Or worse, seeks a younger love in the town
While she with her fading muslin apron
And her dented tin pail seeks greens, always
Greens, and wins, with her intermittent sighs,
Sympathy, love forever, from the boy.
He does not know, this sharp-boned boy who bends
To his mother, that he has been seduced
Already, that he has known anguish, bliss
Of sex — as much as he will ever know.
He does not know, here in the bees' shadow,
that he has become the tall and angry man,
The husband wounding the woman who bends,
Sighs and is ecstatic in her clutching
Of sons — bending, dark of brow, by her pail,
Stooped, brushing back the long, complaining strands
Of her hair. She is now too proud to weep,
But not to read the law, to reap greens, greens
Forever in her small, pathetic pail.

TWO FARM SCENES

i

On the farm this had been the hour
Persimmon leaves rang like iron
Or the sound of the screendoor slamming
Flung itself for two long miles up the hill
Beyond turnstiles, past the laggard cows
To the ear's target where the boy wandered,
Tapping his fresh stick along the path.
Or perhaps the old man's shout caught him
In a beaver brook, where long grasses combed
The mud. Deer too indulged the sliding belly,
Endured chill blessings of the sly and beaver priests
Who raised the waters high over an eager back.

ii

The boy looks up from the long rows of corn,
Startled. He sees the old man as if a horn blew.
Oh why does he fear his grandfather
Grey in the startling sun, beyond silken curls?
Only that that man might bother
To stoop and tell him how years flee,
Delicate and skittish as his pale pony.

X-RAY

Strangely
   my mother's sad eyes
     did not show up
      on the X-ray
though I had long since
   swallowed
     all her sorrows
and they should have been
    right there
      where the pain IS

nor my father's
    old loves
     which should have been
      THERE
   cavorting
heedless of fluoroscopic
     voyeurs

nor was the little boy
   loveless and snotnosed
who'd been entombed
   for sure
     there
   years ago
in sight,

Perhaps he hid
   behind the spleen
      behind the ribs
Oh he is out of hiding now
   and is drumming drumming
      drumming my heart.

MIDNIGHT

The linoleum has archipelagoes of socks
You would have picked up.
My need for your love
Is like an intense, high-pitched
Coded scream that floats out over valleys.
No one sleeping in the farms between us
Can hear this cry for help.
I wonder if you do.
Do you think it is the scream of an animal?

THE CARD-PLAYERS

How we envy their not caring,
        their sculptural crossing of legs,
their idle tossing of cards!
When they get up they are satisfied
as if from work. They rub
                        their hands,
                adjust belts,
jingle change in their pockets, and
see that their wives have been loyal
                in their absence.

ON A FIFTEENTH-CENTURY FLEMISH ANGEL

The toe sticking out from under the hem
Of that angel's blue skirt
Shows, along with the finger raised
In no-nonsense admonishment,
That you are dealing here
With a down-to-earth angel,
An angel whose wings belong, organic
As a bird's: not like those Greco
Angels, sour-faced and grim with doubt.
The face of this particular red-haired

Angel, with blue wings and ruddy cheeks,
Holding a mace he'd use to crack
Your noggin, tingles from the chill
Of northern skies; yet those cheeks
Are luminous with the long light
Of stars. His flesh is warmed
By blood that never need be drained.

A VIEW OF THE VALLEY DURING YOUR ABSENCE

You have been gone three weeks
And I have not yet shipped the clothes
You left in my apartment.
The lights of the used-car lots
Still shine like sprawled garnets
                on the Elmira Road.

ON READING THAT NAPOLEON WAS POISONED

Science has pinned
Napoleon down
At last

Those final days
On St. Helena
The walks, the sea

And those who worried
Scanned Europe
Thought they'd better

Take steps, science
Now confirms, neutron
Analysis shows

From the clipped
Hair of the little
Fellow

That he was poisoned
Slowly
Over a period of time

In his soup
They thought it
Clever, covered up

Wiped off the slates
Of history but
Hair takes into itself

All stories, a man's
Aspirin, his
Arsenic

And you can be
Tested in a thousand
Years

And they will know
Whether
When you turned

To me
Love shot
Through your long hair

FOURTH OF JULY

My uncle,
Great Norman,
Whose leg was full of
Finest German steel,
Broke three chairs and a table
When the kids
Set off firecrackers
On July 4, 1946,
Just after apple pie.

CHIGGERS

On the farm long ago
we all drank from
the same dipper

made of a hollowed gourd —
my grandfather
and my Aunt Beatrice

and my teenage uncle W.T.
who told me three chiggers
would bore through me

then I would die
and even my father drank
from that dipper

before he went back
to the plowing
and when he blew his nose

he held one nostril
and bent over to blow
toward the new, shining

furrow where I followed
tired and eager, afraid
of three red tiny dots

the potash soap
would not wash off my belly
though uncles chanted hope

above the smokehouse tub
steaming under hams
of hogs I'd known by name.

WE WAITED WHILE THE LANDLADY'S SON

went to look for her in the tavern.
he was a fireman
who'd been watching television

by the lake. it was the cottage
on stilts we wanted,
it looked out over the cold

waters and the lapping shadows.
the moon was out there
and would seem ours

if we viewed it from those quilts
and paneled windows.
the walls were cedar

and so hooked around
it was impossible to smell
or see a car.

we'd know the lake
from now on inward,
from a true touch of it,

we were tired of curving
ever landward
but wanted a spot

where we too
could glow and be known
like a docked boat

or wave quietly and shadowed
like a flower.
you wept when he said

Ma don't want to bother
she don't ever change her mind
Ma has closed down for the season

DEATHLACE

With deathlace tickling my throat
I'm bulb-eyed at midnight
To remember whole afternoons of causes
Charley Pape and the '35 Dodge
Opening it up, all those giggling girls
Before I was old enough. That's the past,
Those girls sitting on tavern stools when

Charley stops in to pick them up, revs the Dodge
And roars down his favorite road.
I'm old enough now and have saved nothing
From that year but roads I can't remember riding
Down. And the quaint odor of flyspray
Around my grandfather's clock
With its gilt painting on the face, an ad.
The expressways, with their share
For each taxpayer, share of the modern death.
These are the death-flies hovering
Around my curls, sneaking a bite
At my tense neck of Apollo.
They are not ordinary flies
On the pink stucco. They are put out
By Standard Oil along with green stamps
And dinosaur balloons. They are a part
Of the deathlace. Peering down
Into my fish gullet even now you might fail
To see it, like a fine crochet or Queen Arme's
On a salmon slope in Oklahoma. Highway 66;
I've gulped it there. Deathlace
From Dodge, Ford, Pontiac, Studebaker.
It floated in from downtown one night
So coughing thick I thought it was L.A.'s
Nudist mag and stripjoint slums I was 2 blocks from
Instead of an upstate valley town with a few
Taverns bobbing their blinkers, used-car lots
Wobbling the long red chain

Of Elmira Road. Winter, and everyone leaves
A little deathlace running while buying stamps
Or wandering the dimestore. It's a gift
To children in strollers and to poets
And to fish and the upper atmosphere
And the doctors and shoeclerks have added
Deathlace looking for deathlace or swollen
Metatarsals. But mostly deathlace has been added
Just for fun. Or the profit on the Eastman film.
Charley with the motor running and that girl goosed.

REDBURN'S VERTIGO COMPARED

He once took delight in the main-skysail
But knew it could be more breathless, heavenly —
For moon-sails and sky-scrapers and cloud-rakers
Touch the high winds too. There is no end
To proliferation of fable — canvas and star
A man climbs as he can. And walking
Without you — it never seemed possible —
I know there is no end to woe — by the barn
An old cow is chewing. She can go on chewing
Forever as I can grieve forever
And always a greater grief and a new land.
The heavens are still dizzy with promises.

THIS LIFE

In my next life sons
but in this I am no Laius
Who knew I would bear such a bounty of daughters
girls of slippers and wheat
girls of roses and sighs
even their tears mirror and dew
necessary to my entire enchantment

O this life for daughters only
and they like the hospital roses
come to color suffering, the room
to move the room and this life
which must move from certain times
and certain places
The wounds, what wounds we have endured
before they have come, our daughters
dancing gaily as roses
They can tend warehouses of wounds
bandagewrappers, they will see us out
to the very end and then they will dwell
in the many states, and they shall know sons

DRAGGING THE MAIN

COMING INTO PORTLAND

Now we give up the frogpond and the road
And the spring you leant over naked.
We give up the badlands and all
The waitresses bringing us coffee. We stop
One last time by the side of the road —
Stones and moose-horns
Before we descend into the plains
And the world once more of the rowhouses.
Twice I have thought of the girl in white cowboy boots
Who glanced at me
In Dickinson, North Dakota.

AN EGYPTIAN COUPLE IN THE LOUVRE

Their decision brought them beyond their
Points of contact — her hair on his shoulder
The touching arm and hip, the lost embrace.
They have become an eternal mood no war can touch.
That they loved each other no one ever doubted.
That they walk on together through the centuries
Is an established fact, his right hand
Holding her little fist as he steps out toward
The town they knew. This fierce expression on
Their faces has been arrested in light, on their journey.

THE PASEO IN IRUN

It is like Dragging the Main
        in our hotrods   back home
only it is walking
        under umbrellas   taking the Sunday paseo
about 7 P.M.   in early darkness
        the mother or the aunt showing off
the young beauty   in the light of ice
        cream parlors   the lovers thrilling
to the touch   this only time   each week
It is Sunday   and raining
        this is the paseo   in Irun or Pamplona
they stroll   in pairs   the *novia*
                        and the *novio*
press each other's   wrists
        and take this sight   permitted
of each other's   night   faces
and moving   lips
And girls go   arm in arm
        throwing dark glances
under the expensive umbrellas   and at the corner
        they swing each other around
with joined arms   as at a Square Dance
                to stroll along
once more   nothing
gets accomplished   except
        what is seen   on a face

22

AT THE TRAIN STATION IN PAMPLONA

the girl sitting on the bench and the
man standing above her with his hands
hopelessly in his pockets are having
a hard time of it. His eyes are almost
as red as hers are and he goes on saying
things with a kind of run-down version
of his usual charm. But she's fed up,
and looking between overcoats, toying
with the green umbrella, in a smoke-
filled station is one more way of
keeping from crying. She gets up
to leave with a vengeance. His hand
touches hers, and he makes her smile
once more, using torture. She'd still
die for him. She reads his face again
like a book she's put down a thousand
thousand times. Now she obeys
and steps up onto that wooden train
past numbers painted gold. This
is a train heading through mountains.
When she settles herself by the window
she is already broadcasting to other
men the message of her helplessness.

SOME NOTES ON VIETNAM

I.

Carpaccio saw all this —
         a gang of armed ruffians
falling to it: the arrow in the throat
         the sword in the belly
the knife through the cheek, the left
         hand pulling the woman's hair
to bring her throat to the broadsword.

Even the trees that nobody notices
         seem to writhe away
from the slaughter of the innocents.

II.

What have they brought to the streets
         of Saigon except smog
and for the kids lessons on how to suck?
The booted Green Beret thinks he is
         after all the uphill hero
         of Salerno.
These are the end-of-the-world days
         and that black kite or crow

in a tree in Spain is no bird or iron-
          sculpture, but a dark sign of the end
the spilled radioactive junk, the unconcern.

III.

It is time to honor the old Fascists.
So *Life* looks up Mama Mussolini
and adores her steaming spaghetti.
And the *West Point Atlas of American Wars*
Uses General Paulus at Stalingrad
For its Horatio at the Bridge example.

IV.

The inductees cross the country in one night
so the men and women sleeping in small towns
will not know what a tidal movement
of armed men is flooding the world.
They pay half-fare like college students
and sit dazed over coffee at 3 A.M. waiting
for the next plane. They talk of Saigon
in the men's room, like some girl
they've had — those who have been with her
and those on the way. And the worst is that

they take with them their inability to love.
They do not sense the dark generations
saying things under the rice.

V.

Under the snow old warriors of 1940
are smiling. So they took Stalingrad after all
and cut down all the birches
and made the minds of the people dream of cars.
Now the rivers are beginning to gleam
like rainbows and smell of American oil.

THE WAY WITH DISSENT
(To Senator Morse)

At the edge of town
Is where we take the man who fights
For what he believes. We find the ditch
There among birches. We leave him.

But some of us wander on after
The day's job of murder

And chance to hear some rare bird
On a tree. The bird sings with integrity.

Rare bird, waiting for a better time!
Singing as if he has no time or place
Of his own, to share with the whole town.

Some of us were born in the wrong land
To be war criminals.

LUNCH IN THE CAFETERIA

Ten years after, and still not
            grown into my grave, I sweep
     through the hospital again. Is it true
            friends died here,
            wrote wills in my presence
            in the solarium, while the TV
     looked on oblivious, not even turned down
            for dignity of the occasion, though
     even bathrobes took on the bronze weight
            of samurai brocade, silken and belted.
     Babcock signed like a warrior
            and reached for the cremation papers
            at twenty-four, with flare and a flourish;

                    the old men looked off over roof-
          tops or yawned, and the magazines said nothing
                    though their greased pages lay open like
                    fishmouths. Dolphins should have
                    risen in commentary
                    to his going down to death-sea . . . .

Ten years ago, I worked my way through school, and wheeled
                    the good-humored up and down the hall
                    to cobalt treatments and their deaths. Once
          after strapping Frank Stein in, I watched the
                    nurse as she thought of something else
                    and nudged the cone off-center; no matter the
          trouble they'd gone to to custom-fit
                    his plaster of Paris chin rests and neckbolts
                    on that barber chair. Like me the nurse
was learning and could afford mistakes. For
          Stein it meant a few less months to hear
the doctors and politicians of his time.

And now, ten years later, only the rain drove me in, past
                    the green light of the autopsy room. My unweighed
                    stomach needed lunch . . . descending the dusty
                    stairs once more I saw purgatory
                    faces, those dying and those sad someone else
          was dying. In the line I shoved asparagus along.
                    A woman dropped her purse and picked it up;

stethoscopes dangled like caught fish in creels
from the white pockets of internes, and I saw
the paradisal faces, the crew of sailing men whose
ships death floated.

COMMITTEE

Men have through all ages sat in council
And sometimes around tables, Homeric
Men, and standing men, Indians, and these
Men in their dark ties. We are in a circle
And talking in a circle and making the
Choices of our lives:
        backache,
        the green blackboard,
        the pipe to be chewed,
        the cough drop,
        the bitter lemon,
        the coil of red cellophane
            around the finger,
        Paper Topics,
        sad doodles of cages and zigzags,
        the Regional Report,
        sinus-carrying Nile sludge,
        all the windows closed,
        backache,
        courtyard brick,

a report from the other committee,
the sun moving away as if appalled,
All afternoon on the ship where there is no leader
and the garrulous lap at us like endless ocean
waves, insignificant and tireless.
Sometimes around this magnificent table
Men who have always been dull and defeated
Seem to take on life as they say "It seems to me . . . "
Or "I should think . . . " or "If you ask me . . . ."
Often we get up as if we'd decided where
To send our frogmen or how to scale the wall.
But no one can find a wall or name a sea.

THE WAVES
(For Wesley)

Where the waves show their teeth
            the way Hokusai made them
                        or saw them
You point, just two years old now,
            and say "Here comes another one!"
You speak with particular reverence
                        for just that wave,
Giving me a moment I can take to the next world.

THOUGHTS OF MALCOLM LOWRY

At least I can still tie my own shoes.
"No, dear," said his wife, "put your sock
on first."
Mine still match five days
out of seven.
The Zenith heavenly circle
still blares out Scarlatti
as it did in Chicago
when we suffered,
bought tin pans
in dimestores.
If we heard of a new form
of suffering
— one with the resiny smell
of pines —
we had to have it, then.
Other hells were strung like jewels.
The men wrote, the girls loved.
The beds squeaked, the cats scratched.
Nausea came out in a new edition.
Malcolm Lowry fell asleep
floating on his back in the Bay of Naples,
some womb,
got frightful burns.
No book is worth it and
I wouldn't slit your belly for one.

ON SEEING A MOVIE BASED ON AN EPISODE
FROM PRESIDENT KENNEDY'S LIFE

Tonight we took
the boys to see
PT Boat 1
09 at the
Dryden Drive-In
3 boys in the
Volkswagen and
our daughter of
course. Before that
we had to watch
Bob Mitchum chase
a tiger with
a torch and then
like Wilson in
Hemingstein's best
story steal the
girl indifferent
ly. Jack Hawkins
tried to shoot him
too. The boys sd
this was scary.
In the next car
a man shoved
his girl down in the
seat and had at

her; I turned the
mirror and watched
his shirt going
up and down, it
took about eight
or ten minutes.
Maybe it was
their first time, they
lit cigarettes
then Jack, dead Jack
came on and we
saw him choose his
PT boat, paint
er up and head
for battle. Av
rom had to pee
just then and wd
nt go outside
on the gravel
so we had to
leave. I loved Jack
Kennedy, he
wanted better
for us than these
Drive-In thumpings.
Under the great
stars of Amer
ica there shd

be better. We
were choked on car
fumes; to go down
town wd be worse.
On the way home
we passed trailer
parks, the sad young
marrieds inside
watching TV.
Why shdn't they
give up and hug
in those shoebox
havens, pullman
bunks and porta
ble blue heavens
if they can't walk
out into the
night without get
ting gassed? They know
their dreams are put
to sleep like pups.

THE FAMILY IN THE HILLS

I don't believe in modern times, I believe in those times.
Still the heartbreak, still no view of the sea.
Still the child in the arms, the bare feet, the bewildered
Look away from the sun.
I have not gone forward into the years of light.
I have fallen back into those years.
For the touch of those arms I would have to go backward
Face by face, arm by arm, through a thousand failures.
Why not start at the beginning? With the first sadness.

THE ART MUSEUM

I hated to leave
                Epstein's woman
                        on the stair
And evidence in the Fragonard
                that my son too would
                        have his day
And be gone

Along with the woman I almost
                broke away from my friends
                        to speak to boldly

Outside, the faces of waitresses
               are immortal and in bronze
I get confused and cannot accept
            the passing faces
                  for what they are

THE MID-EVENING ANGST

Just the scraping of a chair
And there's the old feeling
— No home for me here —
And simple questions become something
Heard in the distance, the whine of a saw,
The scare of a plane,
The squall of a child who might turn out
To be really somebody.

Sometimes the door falls a thousand feet
In your hand but there's
No hole to gape at.
Can you still chant the schoolyard
What the hell do I care?
Beyond the toes on the stairs,
The jumping
Of the child waiting to behold you
As you have made yourself to be beheld

(Paterfamilias in a halo of blue
And forget-me-nots along a path)
There is this business of
Their faces coming to a dead stop.

MY DAUGHTER AS A NUISANCE

It breaks my heart
That's how my aunt
Or uncle would
Have said it. I
See her circle
The burdock pile
The dog snapping
At her ribbons.
She stumbles, cries.
All is fever
In the noon sun
In the pitiless
Growing up that
Left me running
In weeds toward my
Father a long
Time ago and he
Turning as if in

Ordinary petulance.
Does that sacred fence
Still stand? I followed
Too close at heel
Into the clearing
Where for once
Bending with hoes
We were united
Hill family
Poorer than poor
With no Kodak
To record our heart-
Break and the strange
Fare of love and the
Lack of love as we stooped
For greens or to destroy
Ourselves in the hills
Where the weeds walled
Us in till we grew tall,
and broke in the sun.

DOING WITHOUT

's an interesting
custom, involving such in-
      visible items as the food
that's not on the table, the clothes
      that are not on the back
the radio whose only music
      is silence. Doing without
is a great protector of reputations
      since all places one cannot go
are fabulous, and only the rare and
      enlightened plowman in his field
or on his mountain does not overrate
      what he does not or cannot have.
Saluting through their windows
      of cathedral glass those restaurants
we must not enter unless like
      burglars we become subject to
arrest) we greet with our twinkling
      eyes the faces of others who do
without, the lady with the
      fishing pole and the man who looks
amused to have discovered on a walk
      another piece of firewood.

HAVING TOO MUCH

shows in more places, not
only the face but the belly and
the polished leather. Wher-
ever you go, round every port
of call, folks who practice
this custom walk with cameras
knocking their knees and
genitals. Like busybodies
they have so many friends to
look in on they can never quite
catch up. They must use
boats, planes, rockets, upon
which they distribute
cigarettes like tickets that
will glow and take you
anywhere, even to the
moon when it opens up
for the season. What they
have learned is certain lessons
which they are fond of
citing, e.g., *money talks*
and they appear to be in despair
from never absorbing quite
enough electricity.

DRAGGING THE MAIN

In the town by the sea I walked
Past the closed beauty shops where the
Hair-driers inside gleamed like bombs
And the mannikins wearing their human
Hair didn't understand this game:
The cars drove round and round the
City blocks, their hoods and trunks
Leaded in and young eyes burned
Like radar above the red fires of cigarettes.

I looked through bakery shops and
Laundromats, searched the stark lights
The put-down baskets, the dizzy doors
For answers. I walked on as they revved
Away. We moved at our different speeds
Through rows of hot-dog stands,
Amusement arcades, pinball games, and doubled
Back. I saw the girl alone
In her car, and she turned to glance
At me. I thought the love that had
Once thrown me away was sneaking up
On four tires and about to say

Honey, you get right in here. I waved.
She sped up and her taillight bobbed

Three blocks away through the mist.
I stopped under the marquee, turned
Again at the Watch Repair
Then saw her eyes again. They were not
Like those floating eyes of fish

That stared from the other cars.
She knew me, but something kept her
From slowing, and made her gawk and appraise.
She was brunette, and all by herself
And passed me five, ten, twenty times.
I waved from the bridge.

Each time I thought I'd lost her
Her gaze honked upon me once more.
Twice in the dark I raced her till
I stood where the Shell sign squeaked.
I breathed deep that perfume she left.
And was glad she helped to destroy me.

More and more she floated past in shadows.
I was chained to her recurring course.
I was faithful. She spoke to me
Lowering for once the window of cold
Glass and we were there by the roaring sea.
She said it wasn't love stinging my face
But only the pure cars of America that
Were dragging the main, looking for fools

Who want to hold even the lights of Main
Street, and the sweetness of a face.

AT THE WASHING OF MY SON

I ran up and grabbed your arm, the way a man
On a battlefield would recognize a long-lost comrade.
You were still wrinkled, and had a hidden face,
Like a hedgehog or a mouse, and you crouched in
The black elbows of a Negro nurse. You were
Covered with your mother's blood, and I saw
That navel where you and I were joined to her.
I stood by the glass and watched you squeal.
Just twice in a man's life there's this
Scrubbing off of blood. And this holy
Rite that Mother Superior in her white starched hat
Was going to deny me. But I stood my ground.
And then went in where for the first time you felt
Your mother's face, and her open blouse.

THE STEWARD

The sixtieth gull.
It begins to rain.
He turns too, in his
White coat, throws
His cigarette into
The sea.
It is time to return
To those who do not
Love him, to babble
Their children
To sleep, to be
Part of the hum
Of the ship's engines.
The nights sail
Away, on the oil
Of manners and charm
But once
They stuffed with wicks
Those white gulls
Of the English Channel
And burned them for
Lamps, when Stuka
Provided the birds
And shore-watchers went
Dizzy. It takes

(This sea where we
Rock) the fieriest
Gulls, and it makes
The Stukas and
Messerschmitts fall
In a mist so thick
Few remember. And it
Gives for a bonus
The calm of white-
Jacketed years.

GATHERING FIREWOOD

CHEKHOV

If I feel that you've
      invaded our privacy,
made our faces sting like nettles,
If I can't find my friends
      or find my life in the dark,
If you've reduced me to tears,
If I know not now
      where to go
        — toward the destructive
        — toward the fragmentary
If you've spoken
      through desperate hands
those vases that break
      those marriages
      those friendships cold
        bitter and lonely,
those partings in the forest,
If I have lost her again and again
I see now,
      Chekhov,
        it is all your fault.

A HILL IN OKLAHOMA

A cellar would keep jars cool.
You promised to dig one.
You could dig one with a mule
And a piece of iron.
But first you had to break the mule
And that was a mean business.
But you kept your vow
And later the mule
Ran away, flipping the iron
End over end
Scaring me like everything
Else you and the mule did.

And she bore jars into the damp earth
Like a Cretan girl.
She placed the jars
Upon shelves that are fallen
Here, all broken in this
Agamemnon's tomb.
And I have come to dig the shards
Out of the wet leaves
And find what you left.
Here are the rusty cans
Our mother fed us from
When she denied the breast,
Small dugs that I remember,

With nipples like figs. .
Here are the rusty springs
Of our bed, both brother
And sister.
And here is a rusty ring
Like a half-moon,
The basin she washed us in.

You were indeed the most cursed
Of parents.
The deep rains hurt at your house
And at last washed it down
The hill.
The open fire in the middle
Of your dirt floor
Burned at your poor bed
Like a rich man's eyes.
In the day you went out and broke
Stones.
The mule learned to turn away
From the ruins
And salt stains on the earth.
And stunned by your own failure
When you left, Christ's life
Ago, you left the gates
Wide open. Iron. Gates.

RAVENNA

And what did we see, high up there
in mosaics
but the old cousins, Beatrice, Edris, Alice
holding cups of gold, their haloes
awkward like the strawhats
they wore in the beanfields

ARCHEOLOGY

I find the old farm,
dig in the ruins, barn,
wagon, smokehouse, caved in
well,
find the rusty three-pronged
pitchfork,
first relic found
that linked Grampa
to the sea.

A RUINED SHACK IN THE HILLS

A man and a woman were up here
in the hills.
They broke rocks.
They broke each other.
They made of the scrub oak
a labyrinth
for finding the bleached bone
of a cow, a pelvis.
And yellow daisies grow,
as over a battlefield.

NOWATA

The town needed me.
It drove me on. Winters,
I slid on the iced rails
Of streetcars.
Summer, I dished stew
Down at the Oasis Grill
and Poolhall, another place
The decent folk
Wouldn't want to look
For love or stew or snooker.
Ah, little did rich old Landers

Know how good that stew was,
Called "Mulligan."
The town needed me,
Desperately.
One June I mowed the whole
Cemetery, then swept the stones.
It's a wonder I didn't build that town.
But I return, and there's still
No town built there
Nor anyone sowing the seeds
Of *Communitas*
On the right side of the tracks.
But I cross over and stare
Where chickens peck
At the ruins of black Myrtle's shack.

THE TOUCHED LIFE

gives up dignity,
cries aloud in public,
gets down on the floor
with the children of light
and of darkness,
weeps openly
or in secret,
yearns for a face

that is gone or
a face in the mirror,
defends the assassin,
sees only glory,
sees no end
to the suffering,
no opening up,
no gifts coming,
finds meaning in wheat,
mostly isn't wanted,
is victim to anything,
a cow, a wooden bucket,
can stand in the doorway
and gawk,
weeps at bikes leaning
together, scrawls notes
madly, shoves them
into books,
is lunatic, wonders
which will come first,
the collapse of
capitalism or the emancipation
of man,
can be a gatekeeper,
can paint plates,
can hear the terrible meanings
go on speaking,
can stand offering spirit
saying would do anything for

and what do *we* do
how do we pay back
the touched life
that spirit pure as
the baby rabbit

by edict saying
it shall not happen
this miracle of
human closeness

AFTER SAPPHO

Let us live so that the rust of our bodies
Will rub off on others, in future years.

THE FAMILY

Rounding up the family one chick
and kitten at a time, I see that even
the fly on the barn wall becomes
someone for whom I was searching

AT THE SPRING

And the sun on her back,
The water so cold. I have forgotten
To love her as I should.
Is there anything quite like the edge of a breast
— like a little moon —
Swinging out at a woman's side
As she bends to the water

NOTE

Dad,
have no feeling for you anymore
can lay your snapshot on the table
and not be moved to tears
your ancient mustache
and the plaid of your sport-coat collar
your slick tie with the wings of herons
I am unmoved

STOPPING NEAR HIGHWAY 80

We are not going to steal the water-tower
in Malcom, Iowa,
just stop for a picnic right under it.
Nor need they have removed the lightbulb
in the city park
nor locked the toilet doors.
We are at peace, just eating and drinking
our *poco vino* in Malcom, Iowa,
which evidently once had a band
to go with its bandstand.
We walk down the street, wondering how
it must be to live behind the shades
in Malcom, Iowa, to peer out,
to remember the town as it was before
the expressway discovered
it, subtracted what would flow
on its river eastwards and westwards.
We are at peace, but when we go into the bar
In Malcom, Iowa, we find that the aunts
and uncles drinking beer have become
monsters and want to hurt us and we do
not know how they could have ever
taken out the giant breasts
of childhood or cooked the fine biscuits
or lifted us up high on the table

or have told us anything at all
we'd ever want to know
for living lives as gentle as we can.

THE INDIANS NEAR RED LAKE

When the white man comes
he comes to see a grave,
to look at the little house
over the grave, to ask
how the dead can eat the food
placed there
and always we give him the same answer
"The same way, white man,
your dead can smell your flowers"

The white man is interested
only in death.
He cares nothing for the story
of the pregnant girls
digging the banana-shaped roots
of the yellow lily
with their toes, tucking one
in at the waist for good luck.

The white man wants to hear
about the German scalp
brought back in nineteen forty-five.
He wants to hear how
it was put on the Chief's grave
After three nights of scalpdance.
He is amused
to think the Chief may stroll
in the other world
with the Germans and the small Japanese
for servants.

He walks through the weeds of our yards
to see a grave.
He brings nothing else, none of the friendship,
the fellowship we've spread our nets for
for years, in our yards,
beside the abandoned Buicks,
waiting for him to notice.

The nets go on catching spiders
and what the white man throws away as
he drives through, fast,
in his car.
We take our smiles to town,
but neither do they catch anything.
Our nets are dry.
Yet we watch them.

AN OLD FIVE-AND-TEN-CENT STORE

It is only nickels and dimes we ring up.
And pennies.
We won't take paper.
Our fortunes must be built entirely
Of pennies and nickels and dimes.
Not a single quarter on the heap!
Not a fifty-cent piece, with the eagle
Of the Republic!
Of human hairnets we have spoken.
Of Mickey Rooney, tinted,
Smiling in tweed
The year he met Ava Gardner
We are discoursing.
Betty Grable we are still propping
On the knickknack,
Looking back at us
Over her shoulder, standing
In her white bathing suit.
Here shoelaces of any length
Are available for the last time!
We are going out of business
Entering the graves
Where ceramic saltshakers will surround us.
We will lie forever on pillows
Embroidered with the names

Of seaside resorts
And verses loud enough to wake us
When we want.

SEASON'S GREETINGS

Sister! And others to whom
I owe this least
obeisance of saying what
movies I've seen
or what I ate for the day
or how the weather darkens,
avoiding politics
and love and the
itchy ass: sisters and
dearest slightest acquaintances
(and mother, and father
who still so strangely live),
please forgive
me — in building
this tiny nest which I make,
this ludicrous, wobbling
nest that barely
keeps me alive,
I have had to steal
all the words

I could get, words
that would never make
sheep, to be herded
into those letters you need.

SKID ROW

Thin curtain bellowing out,
endlessly begging in the night.
And in the morning, the last pennies,
out of a can, for a plum.

ANALYSIS

Here is my great book.
It is called Paradise Lost
(I regain it as I talk)
Naked as jaybirds,
Adam and Eve are all alone,
except for me.
I crawl and see them
from the floor.
At noon my Mom

is always eating.
It might as well
be what I say,
or me.
She talks to Dad
right after. I'm
despised
and might as well
be killed
with a hard hoe
(work came before
sin) The hate
of Satan
is what I know.
My hands are small and wet
with tears.
The telling of this tale
has taken years.

A MIDNIGHT DINER BY EDWARD HOPPER

Your own greyhounds bark at your side.
It is you, dressed like a Sienese,
Galloping, ripping the gown as the fabled
White-skinned woman runs, seeking freedom.
Tiny points of birches rise from hills,

Spin like serrulate corkscrews toward the sky.
In other rooms it is your happiness
Flower petals fall for, your brocade
You rediscover, feel bloom upon your shoulder.

And freedom's what the gallery's for.
You roam in large rooms and choose your beauty.
Yet, Madman, it's your own life you turn back to:
In one postcard purchase you wipe out
Centuries of light and smiles, golden skin
And openness, forest babes and calves;
You forsake the sparkler breast
That makes the galaxies; you betray
The women who dance upon the water

All for some bizarre hometown necessity!
Some ache still found within you!
Now it will go with you, this scene
By Edward Hopper and nothing else.
It will become your own tableau of sadness
Composed of blue and grey already there.
Over or not, this suffering will not say Hosanna.
Now a music will not come out of it.
Grey hat, blue suit, you are in a midnight
Diner painted by Edward Hopper.

Here is a man trapped at midnight underneath the El.
He's sought the smoothest counter in the world

And found it here in the almost empty street,
Away from everything he has ever said.
Now he has the silence they've insisted on.
Not a squirrel, not an autumn birch,
Not a hound at his side, moves to help him now.
His grief is what he'll try to hold in check.
His thumb has found and held his coffee cup.

MOVEMENTS

Country —
making a museum out of walking around,
porcelain dogs, rusty bridge
of old Korean bronze,
windmill that turns, Uffizi
ditches
and Prado tar —
with pieces torn out of my own life.

Town —
making a museum out of driving around,
hot-dog stand so hot it burned down,
McDonald fine orange wickets,
billionth burger of the economy,
and plenitude of wild dimestores.

W.C.W.

knew a poet
doesn't have to be on
his best behavior

all the time, has
many bad
poems, very
lifelike, very

relaxed, and breaks
into song
only on occasion

as all folks do,
walking along

MY POEMS

are like cedar shakes
which I let slip
from my fingers
one by one
in the middle of the ocean

THE ARCHAIC

If something is archaic
    all edges have been dulled
broken by the sea
and yet
some trace
    of the old life
        must be left,
some evidence that this white stone
    was once a lion's
        leg, or the base
of an intricate temple.
If that life
    surviving wind and sea
does not lead
    us back, in some effort
to rediscover, retracking
    our own steps,
        then this something
we have found
    in its desolation
        is not truly
            archaic.

To be archaic
    is to exist
        in a state of transition

between a silent life
    and a whispering death:
        even our own
bodies when we stop and
    listen closely
        seem to be giving off
some aura
    of the genuinely
        archaic.

IN GREECE

Approaching that fantastic
space behind all men and women
(still holding their stone robes)
you see that there is only one
relationship; two figures in the
foreground, one range of mountains
in the immense distance, with
nothing in between.
Are you sure you can face it?
Here we have our pain —
our candles, and a dark sea,
our faces growing white like statues.

WITH SAMUEL

We ignore the barbed wire
from an old war.
The donkeys bray all night.
My son is the first man
to see the holy moon,
the wrinkled sea
that will shipwreck
no saint tonight.
"It's the right moon," he says.
He is my friend.
I lift him high, so high.
A few flowers survive.

AT DELOS

I have come to protest
above the empty treasury shaft,
the deep quarry where they came,
and I stand before the archaic holy
lions with their round jaws
and take the sign out of my pocket,
unfold it, hold it up
and let them see it, let them

read my placard — it is written
on the back of an old valentine —
Now I am moving down the line
of old emperors,
bearded, whipped by rain,
their faces enduring in tobacco-
colored marble,
half fallen into the sea,
here where even the winds turned round.

THROUGH MUSEUM GLASS

Bronze greaves of 5th century
B.C.
I still have knees for

DISCOVERING OLD HOTELS

We are not the first
to put time on this room
wash in their sink
put love into
this bed

and walk across
these creaking floors.
Such furniture
as this
the politicians
forgot to axe and
in the red light
of the fire exit
we hear voices drifting
over the transom
talking of wars
that are gone
so we can sleep
a little

THE NEW WIDOW

The new gloves, veil,
smile that is tempered in an hour.
Black hand pushing past fruit,
a woman runneth over
out of this darkness.

ADA

We find her on a sidestreet
of Sapulpa, living
in a little tomb her son
built of stones.
We walk in, under
the catalpa tree, and
she cradles our faces
in her hands,
asking where we've been.
"I'll cook for You-uns," she says,
knowing we came for the old days,
knowing we can see reflected
in her eyes
the clock and the day-bed
and the fields through
the window, with cousins
stooping there.

In the front bedroom where
she slept with Grampa
the dog with the chipped ear
listens.
The stove blazes through isinglass.
We have found for a moment
this woman with her hair
in a bun, who stood with Grampa

before a giant wooden wheel
that never went anywhere,
while we hopped round like chickens.

IN HERAKLION

When we counted out the few coins in our purse
at the hotel desk
and found out we had enough to take a bath
they did not guess what riches we took with
us (hidden in your coat, hidden in
me) up the stairway
and what laughter we surrounded ourselves with
(all by ourselves)
when we sank down to the floor by the radiator
trying to get warm
turning to each other because the radiator
was cold, because only hair warmed me.
That day, or the day before, we had sat
upon the throne of Minos — first me
then you.
We rode the bus back from Knossos.
We bore the faint mark of the king
upon our passports. We walked through
the mobbed streets of that city
built for Hercules. We smelled

the hot foods, the lamb they were cutting
and no one guessed I was luckier
than that king who was not in love
so they didn't try to take you away
from me and it was easy
to pay for a room and watch my
princess sink into the ancient pool.

THE BLUE DUCK

An idea can be glazed, captured, brought down
From heaven!
Our feathers can become blue,
Even a beak can smile!
This duck crouches in a world that cannot
Break it, says Open our eyes,
Let them become luminous,
Amused, and kind!
Duck says to so much: I am not interested.
Duck says Let us feel this blue floating
Down from heaven, let us have thoughts
Between us, let us be fearless.
Duck says Consider the dumbness of animals,
How wonderful it is not to care about death,
To go on falling away from this worst nature

That has been patted upon us like clay.
Duck says We can sit still and go on swimming
Toward the infinite.
Duck says We do not have to judge
With pleasure or displeasure or tell
Ourselves it is all for the best or not.
Duck shows us how naked he is,
How obscene it is to wear a helmet.
Duck says, even to Sunday crowds,
We are lovers, we are without purpose!

JUDY, A FACE

The face is a
constant; the distances
are forgotten and then
attack again, make
themselves known;
it is quite
literal
the elevation, the
inches
I am above
a face, and the waves
that lie between me

and a face.
My mind
knows the outlay
of miles
and minutes, and how far
the light has fallen
into darkness.
This is the face
always framed
in the hair
or by light only
or by air itself
or by the future's
unfortunate
wooden frame; it is a
face, the face
across the sea;
it is all the structure
hands have been
searching for,
what archeologists
have been trying
to cradle in their hands,
for they have searched
for nothing else
not even in the lakes
of Africa;
and this is what it is

— a face —
what music tries
to find, what the makers
of plots
must weave around;
this face is
the only thing time
has worked
to bring
into the light
and into my hand, a face

GATHERING FIREWOOD

This too is a way
of making love, saying
nothing, breaking the sticks
over our knees,
seeing that the green moss
of graveyards is the greenery
of our fire, mingled
eyes. The geese are white
as your blouse. These sticks
cannot be used to beat
us black and blue and tear

our image down all night.
We are breaking them over
our knees, once in a while
smiling

ENOUGH OF FLYING: POEMS INSPIRED BY THE GHAZALS OF GHALIB

All one night when you tried to leave me
I saw the most terrible shapes.
I didn't know you were only trying.
That was the worst night of my life,
the most terrible spaces, falling through them.

As I said, move nothing, not even your hands.
Let the jug and the wine stay equally silent
While we hear our dark breath
                              coming darker, together.

Why did you come here
if not to hear that terrible
explosion of first our hands
then our hair, our eternal hair

I have had enough of flying.
It is to the dust of the streets now
I'd like to descend.

Almost in love
          I think so

now that we have burned
          and eaten forty nights
broken windows with whispers

If you appeared
surely these pines would become water

Love justified, love worth its hell,
tell me more.

Something terrible will come of our love.
Some cock with wings.
Some broken angel.
Some terror to both men and women.

We were whipped with our own hair,
beaten with the palms of our hands,
Four of them.
This is what it is like, becoming saints.

Feel the world tremble through us,
not even us. Feel the world tremble.

Leave the wine. Touch nothing,
not even touching.

Flee from me.
I am mad. I am aflame.
All the fields of me are burning
because you have hurt me, because
you have kindled me,
with that secret fire.

I create no poems.
I write them out
merely to destroy their terrible life.

When there is a terrible heaviness
Some feather breaks.

I prayed for death.
He wouldn't come once.
But a thousand times, oh ten thousand came.
And yet not once.

In heaven I would want to be back here,
fighting with you,
this inexplicable rage.
Only a lover knows it, only a lover

After fifty years I would still see
rose tips, eyes going suddenly soft

How can we recover our strangeness
to each other?
Let us go back to that time
before the battle was won.
Can you tear up my note again
and act as if you mean it?
You did that so splendidly!
You were so indignant!

The path you usually took
was empty that night.
I stood and watched the sea
through the almond blossoms.

Thank you for making me suffer.
Out of that suffering
has come all that I know.

Going to meet you I saw a girl
with a suitcase full of stones.
I should have helped her.
She disappeared down the street
of brothels, where the lamps
dangle in the wind.
This was in Barcelona.

Ghalib — greybeard, metaphysical tailchaser.
And I too find my beloved at every corner.
I rarely speak — just like the master!
I do all my suffering alone.
Or perhaps he did it in a different way.
I'll give him credit.
Some lightning hits the ground.

My love made her younger by the moment.
His genius had left her broken, half dead.
With me she discovered her wings.
And the flower of her mouth, the dark rose
of her belly, the worry of her flanks.

It is not enough that a flower in the street
greeted her.
I too was supposed to fall at her feet.

The wind took her
because I could not.

And my talents are as nothing
because they waste, they wither.

If I'd received her name from her lips
at least I'd have a mantra.

CONFESSIONS OF A HAPPY MAN

I have come to tell you
I am the music of my own defeat,
It is almost breaking
                me.

How do you stay
And not seem to be destroyed
By these voices, these waters
                washing round you?

I am the sound of my own defeat,
Neither the flower nor the song blossoming.
I am neither the curtain nor anything
in the room.
I am not a made thing, not a shelter,
Not a note of music,
            Surely I am not the tapestry
Nor anything fine.

You sit, so absorbed, so oblivious,
As if apprehension had left you long ago,
Made you sit like a silent sea that will never more
Endure a storm. You have created
Some new and original simple-mindedness;
Some ecstasy before which my longing must
Bow down. Even your curls are an invitation
To matters far and long. Your dreams? Yes
Now I see this,

You are set upon by dreams, pinned in
Their golden light, like Saint Sebastian
And his arrows. You sit like a fantastic
Roman saint caught in a wood that survives.
You sit dazed by dreams
            you've stolen from night.

Whether you have wisdom or merely appear to
Is something I worry about as I travel on.

So I remember your eyes and try to think
On their quality of round seeing.

These are the concerns of years now, of years.
And yet of wisdom you will tell me nothing.
Is it a path worth pursuing?
Is it the deception of a simple child?

When you smile I think we are wholly occupied
With the affable. I dream of going back
To worlds we've left, before I oppressed
The ocean, scarred the sky,
And made myself a pain to women. I look
Over your shoulders
And watch the stars burning, finding in
Them more friendliness, more loneliness.

After Ghalib's Ghazal XXIII, translated with Aijaz Ahmad

THE TRAMP'S CUP

THE MONASTERY IN SCOTLAND

You notice
everything, the way thought
smells, the oatmeal and honey menu,
brocade pillows one kneels upon, how
a fly crawls (he may be
incarnate

and selfless
himself), and the drop of
water warping the floor floats higher
with each mantra and is as crucial
as the lines in a face
fate has told

us to look
on here by a Scottish
stream. Kneeling by pebbles, the lady
says, is a way of overcoming
Brooklyn and cancer, and
helps forget

oily eyes
one has looked upon, loved.
In the humming sunlight we are weep-
ing together, arms about ourselves
blessing the dragonfly
who loves us

and then we
drink tea, in our guest shack.
We lie down meditating, admit
we cannot find peace, and must leave off
wisdom to search for joy,
opinion,

the edge of
a window. Once more your
eyes take me back, nowhere else can I
truly be at home who am not wise —
nor elsewhere be alive
at all. How

close I am
to you, yes, I am crawl-
ing upon you now. I am the fly,
the dragonfly, skimming, suffering,
I am the waterdrop.
I am you.

COUSIN ERIC
(For Judy)

Their planes looked like dragonflies
and they flew with the same hushed innocence.
And when one fell in flames outside Dusseldorf
after leveling an apartment building and ripping
craters in a playground
he created a small fire of grief
that would burn in a cousin's eyes.
Cousin Eric had been shot down over Dusseldorf.
And there thirty years later
a wind-broken dragonfly falls
through the open window of the train
and onto the velvet seat.
He is Cousin Eric, I am sure.
This fact which my heart knows
makes as much sense as the others,
explains the flame still burning in your eye.

THE GREATEST POEM IN THE WORLD

Once, in Crete,
I was asleep near the sea.
The room was cold

and I woke with the greatest poem
ever about to be written in my head.
I heard waters running under stone.
Searched for a light, searched
for a fire, nothing.
Shivering, I wrote the poem
on the sheet, in the dark.
It was a great poem,
and first thing in the morning,
to celebrate,
I ran out and took a swim.
It was marvelous to have written
the greatest poem in the world.
It summed up everything.
On the way back from the sea's
great reward and kiss of me
I saw the women
doing laundry in a huge boiling
pot, three women. They had already
washed away the greatest poem in the world
with their greatest pot in the world.
And I hadn't memorized it,
the sea had taken it.
And I stood weeping in the smoke,
wind hitting the caverns in my head.

A DANCE ON THE GREEK ISLAND

The music is mournful, the light
catches a woman's face
under the plane tree. Now the animal
becomes well-integrated; faces,
shoulders, become vertebrae;
hands on shoulders make one animal hopping
to the strings, and the moon
is rising, as it should
for the scene to be fantastic.
Now each man has found his love,
even where to hop, and our body
strolls until the tail
flops like a thumping, ribboned dinosaur's.
The tourists have welded themselves
on, and with a bump and a grind
have offered themselves up
to the Greek religion; they are the tail
end of an ancient rhythm. They have
shaken loose and have lost their towns
and are trying to discard
their wild souls. The girls are shaking
spirits from their hair while the old
lean upon the backs of chairs
and watch for mistaken matings, and at last

the flutist steps through shadows
and runs around us chasing
first one and then another of our bones.

OLD POSTCARDS

A bargain was it not? This stack
of postcards, sepia, showing
French towns after the first attack
sunlight on bombed buildings glowing
and ink script saying of one town
after another "They shot down

The planes that did this filthy work
but the damage was far far worse
than the picture shows." In the murk
near a stream lies a Belgian horse
whose brothers pull the German carts
piled high with somewhat more than hearts.

"We live about a mile from here"
a postwar man wrote in blue ink
and drew an arrow pointing where
his "chateau" could be found, with pink
flowers growing in the craters, tall.
And that cathedral did not fall.

WORDS AT MIDNIGHT

How often when some barber's put a dirty towel
against my head and his thumbs caressed my neck
with some sense of how tired and hopeless
my life has been (barber studying that *Retrato*
in his mirror) have I suddenly — looking out
through double doors — seen a busy restaurant
or hat shop or *super-mercado* and thought of you,
my barber father, your life shuffled out
around a barber chair, like Samson at his mill.
The more foreign the place, the more likely
I'd think of you, for you are strange and alien
always to me. The Mexican who trimmed my hair
tonight was father for a while. His scissors
clicked away on this eve of Independence Day
when the Niños Heroes fought at Chapultepec.
I've never been a man for fireworks,
and yet if after all these years I'd really gain
my freedom, from you and your ever-present
absence, I'd yell and throw fire everywhere.
A tender touch is a service — in Barcelona
I thought of you, and resented the clipping
of my curls, knowing, if it were you, you'd
want to cut me down, and trim my very soul.
I still feared those times you'd really cut
me up, and left me more than once, at least
an ear gone. But now, as if anaesthetized,

I feel the last hair of youth falling,
while the barber says *"Mas corte? Mas corte?"*
He's Samson at *his* millwheel. And no doubt
to others, you gave such tenderness, such welcome
ministrations, obsequies. No doubt gave
to others ample love, so long as they were not
your sons. And maybe they tipped and maybe
they didn't. And now it's midnight and time
to find the park where Catherine wheels
are burning. (Remember that? It was the name
of my pathetic mother.) A life's a life
so long as hope for change can send us
running, for a haircut or the alameda fireworks.
This you somehow knew, and so, Dear Dad, do I.

MISSOURI WEDDING

Stained glass in the old church struck by
the day's last light ricocheted from
fields of wet timothy and weeds
at eight P.M. was heavenly
as if God could after all care
about the generations of
this silly family, three now
sad and sorry. Sour. Sister's
son now a groom, though it seemed just

yesterday that Sis herself stood
at such an altar. Thus gloomy
thoughts, while no one looks around, but
inspects new hats. Funereal
despite the prim, cute, on-their-best
behavior twin nephews in their
tuxedoes at the door, ushers
whispering us to oaken pews,
shushing the yet younger, who looked
like extra pumpkins sprung up on
vines, with lots of yellow tassels.
Musty, sad, this varnished chapel,
despite the theme of joy, licensed.
And we'd arrived in rain, and just
on time, as if these vows concerned
our love and not these two sudden
effusive children, standing there.
Then the bride and her two sisters
dolled in pastels, in huge straw hats,
burst, bounced, into a song, teeny
boppers trilling, wildly singing
And There Is Love. And There Is Love.
(I was glad to hear.) The preacher
was appalled. I loved them then, saw
from my birdwatcher's pew that they
loved, like birds, bright species new here
to our breed, female's eyes dilate
on the male's, emitting mating

calls. And yet, familiar too, from
our loving. Plump robin redbreasts?
Hummingbirds leaving home, with wings
vibrating? Mud-loving phoebes
about to build adobe homes?
Shy larks? Wild canaries singing
"Dearie, Dearie, hear me, hear me"
sparrows who'd like to nest on ground?
The male stood awed. But I could feel
the deep throes of hurt still within
those present who all their lives had
feared love, who found revelations
like this song's cause for pushing back
thoughts of kisses hard to come by.
I saw my mother blush. And yet
this pair were three-fourths married then.
I felt the triumph of their song,
these rouged, swaying girls painted up
like walkons for the burlesque stage.
Later, in the concrete basement,
Aunt Ruth bragged on about the gifts —
"See that blanket. I gave it to
them, and three other presents too."
As if they needed any but
their own hot stuff to keep them warm.
Aunt Ruth ate the white cotton cake
and sat across from Uncle Harold,
a pair of Cezanne's card-players

perched at a tiny wooden table
by the door. She could not believe
the center stage was not for her,
she who'd left the shack of a marriage
burning, who'd wrestled my own father
on a rotten porch for a gun,
whose talents were her tongue of flame,
her tiny feet, her face that made
her once a high school beauty queen.
To see her thus subdued at last
was strange. I marveled at it,
borrowed the nephew's camera.
The groom's father hit the other
twin for eating mints too soon.
The groom wiped shaving cream
with his finger off the wedding
car, and tried to find the culprit.
The bride threw her bouquet of roses.
Her weeping roommate in purple
slacks jumped, caught it. And the newly
weds sprang into their middle age
just as their tires peeled off, away.
I cannot say how that boy looked,
like one of Stendhal's bureaucrats,
with paunch and handlebar mustache,
already older than his father.
Two weeks later he became a cop.

We crossed a bridge to get there.
We crossed another to get back,
rusty iron bridges deep in oaks.

UNDERSTANDING POETRY

Buffalo Bill
        by e.e. cummings
is on page 50,
        I can never find it
        right before class
when girls are biting
        their fingernails
and looking out the window
        with classic boredom,
and we are going to discuss
        Buffalo Bill
                by e. e. cummings
and why he uses the word
        defunct
                for Bill
                        instead of
                                dead
                                passed away
                                kaput
                                kicked the bucket

went on to the happy
hunting ground

and whether or not it's
a better poem
than Trees
by Joyce Kilmer.

TO ONE WHO IN HIS LOVE OF LIBERTY
LEAPED FROM THE STATE CAPITOL DOME

Oblivious —
the traffic roar,
the creaking boughs,
the whistling winds
through parking lots,
miles of tarmac
for what we love.
Perhaps you thought
we'd notice or
bother stooping
to comprehend
your tragic life —
not a chance, it
isn't done! State

senators are
on their way to
walnut chambers
for something else,
more laws about
the motor car;
natural gas
rates need fixing.
Your dance above
their polished tiles,
your fall through air
was nothing but
a nuisance, waste
of your time, theirs.
Yet there was wit
in your gesture,
terrific leap
within the dome
that lifts up high
Dame Liberty.
You had a mood
that needed out,
affirmed. You raised
your hands above
your head, they swore,
the janitor
passing by, tour
guide too. You sailed

beyond them, left
the town where girls
beat you with curls.
Held your arms arched
as if you took
one into the
ghostly air, to
float and gloat, burn
through the bronze torch
that bums can see
from a park bench.
With one lone phrase
you emptied out
yourself, so much
more cleanly than
we can do, who
pick our verbal
asses. All we
are turns into
words. You did it
cleanly, brooded
for a year, then
fell, in one poem.
No matter if
no audience,
save one. I heard
you, friend, I heard.

"TAKE ME BACK TO TULSA"
— *Popular Song*

I am taken back to Tulsa
and taken to a banquet in my honor
in a fine hotel with gilded mirrors
and red velvet drapes, where darky waiters
light the candles by our steaks.
All this, and oil-rich families
regarding lobster as nothing special,
must have been here, just like this,
when I was small, two miles away,
tears on my face, looking toward
these stone buildings, floodlit
all the rainbow colors.
No one brought me in to eat, then.
No one asked me how I felt.
The pillows of the bed were damp all night.
The floodlights changed their colors
till the dawn and even then, the mind
looked back, to sleeping on the floor
down at the farmer's market,
wood planks, tin roof,
waiting for light when Dad would sell
the melons we had grown
(he'd beaten me for hoeing some
instead of weeds).
Visiting Sundays when no one came,

no mother's steps beyond the beds
of flowers, in sun
that melted tar until it ran.
and rich folks were escorted through
like tourists, with adolescent girls
staring at us while we washed like Jews
(a dozen of us naked in a shower)
and in the distance, day and night
we heard the tom-tom dancing of mad Indians
who hugged the hills and crouched in valleys.

POE'S ANVIL

At the drive-in theatre where they sell junk
on Sundays we saw a man and his wife standing
by a pick-up truck trying to sell his anvil.
It sat up in the truck's bed — it was black,
heavy, and elegant like a mammoth's tusk.
And his name was written on it like a signature,
in iron that once ran like ink. His name was Poe.
I talked with him and he recalled briefly
days when his anvil stood outside a shed,
a workshop like a harbor set in a sea
of green tomato fields, and inside
he had a coal fire and a bellows and he watched
the tractor replace mules and the car

replace wagons. He tired of horse-shoes,
wagonwheels and plows, of hitches, barrows,
and lugs, of axles, crankcases and flywheels,
and he sat somewhat amused (and dying, his wife
told us), presiding over the sale of his own
monument, which he wanted someone to go on
hammering on, and in the midday city sun
the theatre's white screen was blank
like a faded quilt or Moby Dick's stretched skin.

SNAPSHOTS

all the generations are on the table
corpse piled upon corpse
tender face we knew
spilled out of a valentine box
and new generations   faces
between us and them
those we loved
calling for attention
still from the grove
or the stone
or the fender —
the wheel unmoving, the oaken
spokes that carried
them nowhere, the man

and the woman
the hand clenched forever —
the young feeling sorry for
our sorrow
saying how sad to be so old
and it must be terrible to have
to drink so much —
so that we pick up these snapshots

SCENE IN CALABRIA

I was concentrating on the child
so I did not hear them.
The child was being born and no one else
on the hill was making the effort.
Sure, the mother was.
But she was alone, with a midwife
who turned out to be incompetent,
with a midwife who let the baby die,
with a midwife whom the doctor lectured
for her stupidity, with a proud, well-dressed
midwife who carried a big leather
purse and drove an Alfa Romeo,
with a midwife who smiled the same way
when she came out as she smiled going in.
She drove the Alfa Romeo

past the boys and the tin cans
and the cindery coke from a thousand
years of blacksmith shop,
and the toothless boys stood and stared
and the sooty-feathered chickens scattered.
In that high room on the hillside
the mother was alive and weeping.
Fra Angelico would not paint this one.

A SWEDISH POSTCARD

If I had been that child tugged up
by the hand onto a streetcar
labed ORMALMSTORG (old grey post-
card), I would recall the bones of
the hand, and the plane trees we bust-
led through, and the face under the
hat with its wide, pink ribbon. There!
I would have said, that's Swedish grief
enough. But as it was, my hell-
fires burned out on a flat, salt plain.
No one spoke Swedish, or sang it,
but when we went to town we lurched
and swayed past quarries where trolley
lightning struck blue and gold. I know
that streetcar well, its wicker seats
and what they said while I hid like

Jonah in the whale. "We'll find one
in Coffeyville," Aunt Bea told her,
"I know we'll find one, I have this
name." I can feel for their tired feet
on the cobblestones, sit with the
two women (ribbons in their hats)
as they had coffee in the bank
building, comforting each other
with low, cooing words. My mother
nearly screamed, sitting near the thick
black vault turned into a pantry
where bullets fired by bandits lay
bedizened in the walls where four
Dalton boys had been shot down like
deer for daring to rob that bank.
Yes, share their disappointment, poor
girls, as they headed home downcast.
When I refer to it now it's
to *my* abortion, though strictly
speaking it would have been my poor
mother's. On the streetcar, going
back from Coffeyville, my small de-
lighted soul heard for the first time
something like Swedish music — high
screech of rails and crunch of polished
fingernails pressed tight together.

VINCENT

It was the wind,
the mistral,
that drove him mad.
At night he painted
the stars —
"Why should
these points of light
in the firmament,
I wonder, be less
than the dark ones
on the map
of France? We take
a train to go
to Tarascon . . .
and we take death
to go to a star."
His friend
had left,
and at night
he painted
those stars,
with candles
in his hat, light
for light,
more stars still
to some God

who watched
with magnifying
eyes. In the town
below, candles
burned on
table tops.
He dare not ask
what others
studied, felt.
His friend
had left, leaving
only the sun
flowing
into the fields,
the sower, the chair
with its candle.
Ignorance burned
like an effluvium,
a gas that kept
the damp town
vicious. Two
francs for
the Hiroshige,
his own
sunflowers a prize
for drinking
beer. And he left
for me as if he were

my father
(and my father had
left me something)
one blossoming
twisted tree
I found
in Manchester
when I went in
from rain when
they had no use
for me and it
was there, a gift
from Vincent,
in brotherhood.

HAMMERING

*"And the last tap of the hammer is worth less
than a* perutah."
                                    — Maimonides

His ultimate
contribution
to the world
he decided
hammering it
in would be not
only the nail

but when driving
the yellow car
moving his right
clenched fist
from steering
to his ear
a subtle
wave which the next
driver seeing him
barreling down
the expressway
would ape
unconsciously
thus passing
the signal on
until soon
through concrete
arteries of
the republic
upon corpuscles
of rubber his wave
would reach
California
and be lost
in the sea
like a smile
offered to strangers
such a life's work
being harmless
he opined

and giving the
universe
something to
detect when it
decides to
get sensitive
to small and exquisite
gestures

MUMMIES & OTHERS

Once Philip IV scared hell out of himself
having the tombs opened so he could see his ancestors,
his gramma, grampa, cousins, a lady or two.
Many died young in those days, diphtheria, wrath,
even the son who'd helped him review
the troops along the river, feathers
on their hats waving in the wind.

But I don't have to go to the Escorial.
The mind does quite a good job, thank you very much,
bringing them all back, misshapen, bulb-
eyed, hag-breasted, so they can scare hell
out of me, the living dead, like the mummies
of Guanajuato if you prefer Mexico
where your cousins and mine, these inamoratae,

twist and writhe, Old World, New World,
what the hell, they writhe.

GENITORI

"And we are the commotion born of love."
— Charles Madge

As a Buddhist tried for months
to visualize a small gold Bodhissatva on the air,
I benignly conjure up this couple,
his arms about her, free of trouble.
They're young and smiling, apple clean,
whose embraces gave my shining hair,
and she is both his piano and his cello,
which are played with fingers, light
arpeggios now and then, rough gutsy
rubbing of the belly when it's night
and how well I know, in cold December
the poor lived better, in glowing embers
of their kindling crates, than we did
wrapped in our clawed-up gramma's quilts.
In the decades later they still obsess us
so that daily we forgive them and daily
don't, and in a field may find them still,
blue in paired flowers, their love transposed

119

and borne beyond a billion rocks, and time,
or caught within a cave by those
who knew them before us, suffering sister,
who wept in the Oklahoma night.
Their best and worst I sing, no longer hate.
And I smile to see my mother still,
cradling the steaming soup, straight down
the hill, to the wretched poor who huddled there
while we at home, brother, sister, sucked the bloody air.

MARRIAGE

There could be a good husband
and a good wife and a bad marriage
all in one, a woman thinking
she could have this or have that,
a man infected with the latest idea
or the other wanting nothing
or wanting each other but at separate
times when the other's loneliness
is not clawing, it is more fantastic
than charting the many ships
and planes coming into the busiest
harbor or port, this business
of the man and woman somehow
landing together, somehow managing

another flight, right on schedule.
And what a port! — sometimes in high
winds not just planes, ships but
balloons, dirigibles, kites, trucks,
covered wagons, all to be secured.

THE INTERVIEW

The way husbands and wives
should be interviewed is this:
in their dance costumes,
holding each other up, I mean
high up, over our heads,
not any of those feet
on the leonine head; putting
their best positions
forward, so to speak,
then leaning on the mantel
giving a word or two
of cosmic philosophy
that makes spiders, small flakes
of snow fall off
their brows, not sitting
like strangers in a bus station
before the lady carries

down the street her ears
and curls in a hat, the man
his eyelids in his fists.

THE TRAMP'S CUP

"I will rise
from my troth
with the dead,
I will sweeten my cup . . ."
    —H.D.

Easier said than done,
a thousand poverties come home
daily
to beg what spirit
we have, to incite old
evil burning on
in the bones,
and I am asked to do it
without wine.

Once, in Yorkshire,
a tramp came begging
to our damp brick farm,
his life's possessions
in the baby's pram
he pushed along hedgerows,

talking to sheep.
We gave him tea
and watched him settle
down for the night
in a grass-lined ditch, wind
blowing over him,
stars burning clear
above him
as he chuckled and sipped
the cooling tea,
pulling over him the frail
tent he'd made, using the pram
for a North wall.

I know why he laughed,
felt free.
All one really needs
is to keep out
the damp.
He had learned that well
and had not an enemy
in the world, had nothing
to fear, nothing
to lose, nothing
to stop loving him.
And thus his cup of tea was sweet.

ORPHANS

MULBERRIES

I brush into a pile
the fallen mulberries,
good for nothing but to make us
slip and break our bones,
and so I give them to my youngest
trees, to my linden and my birch,
to nourish them.
I never want my children
to eat mulberries,
because once upon a time
I had to live on them,
sitting with my sister
in the branches. We were
bitter, having nothing else,
nothing save hate,
which we work now
into proverbs, as I sweep
into a pile the fallout-
dusted berries
which are good for nothing
in modern times
though the Chinese found them
first-rate for paintings
on silk, and children once
took them into their bellies
with defeat.

ORPHANS

In Ireland they were put in foundling homes,
so many sprung up after the great potato blight,
mothers left them in the fields, after they'd scratched
the earth up, or on doorsteps . . . and the beadles took them
into the foundling homes. There ninety percent died
in their first year for lack of touch.

The final insult is to be dragged into the orphanage
screaming "I'm not an orphan." Not as it should be,
with the orphans, who have nothing, on the bottom
of the heap. Quite the contrary, it is they
who proudly look down on the non-orphans, whose parents
have judged them unworthy, who still live in the city
nearby, who could save them if they cared.
You see that skyscraper, the one with the lights
that change all night, the colors of the rainbow?
That's where your mother lives and works and has her
boyfriends, Jim, Gary, Gerald, bedspring-
squeakers, huggers, tiptoers, laughing
at her question, "Did you forget the rubbers?"
Your mother, man, would spread her legs for any man
who asked, while joking in the hospital that you
needed no privacy, being too little for all that.
So they took away the only screen you had
and let you cry in public while someone else's roses
wilted in the sun.

In the orphanage the inmates fall in love, and Juliet of the
    sorrows
turns twelve and is taken off like a dog
to be put in still another home, the Francis Willard,
down a dusty road. They'll let you ride along
if you won't scream, and see her in the door
where she will lie quietly as if strapped down
and let her breasts grow and keep secret your vow
to meet at twenty-one, under the clock, at noon,
and love forever and hate them all.

Donald, whose gramma came on Christmas and gave him
an apple, the only thing she had, is the only kid
with pubic hair. Together
all of you take a shower in a huge stall
and Nazi ladies in fur coats
are escorted through to look at you; one girl
of twelve is lovely and she stares. It could
be love, but it's only more shame, and hate.
The rich who care and have each other
are strolling through
and smelling clorox and wondering what
they'll give this year, the girl stares
as if you're almost human. Her mother drags her on.
Donald fights. The boys cut pictures of their fathers
out of *Life* magazine. They're fighting, too, in jungles
overseas. Christ knows who a father is.

The matrons are chosen because they can wear
the white uniforms with thick starch —
polar regions, talcum, annihilation.

Their eyes are always angry, ready
to carry out the Court's will, be it
Death or Neglect.
They enjoy hurling the miserable child
down stairs, hearing him weep in the night,
enjoy making him eat turnips or whatever
makes him throw up, enjoy cutting the blonde
girl's braids, throwing them into the toilet,
reminding her that no mother wants a lock
of that hair to save. They enjoy pinching
the small buttons of the girl's nipples,
enjoy stuffing bananas up her quivering
cunt, they enjoy shouting "Nobody loves
you, nobody, not even yourselves,"
enjoy beating them, then saying "Sit down
by that fire escape and learn your
multiplication tables," enjoy kicking them
black and blue and livid and mottled red,
enjoy sending them to school like a chain
gang, all dressed in corduroy any cop
can spot should they break away and run,
up the tarmac road, begging at motorists.

And like a co-conspirator the blue-dressed

headmistress with stars on her bosom
has shaken hands with the pathetic
abandoning parent. What did she say
that last time, before stepping over barbed wire
to be gone forever? *So long. Be good. I'll write.*

The murdering matrons greeted orphans
as equals, credited them with killing
off that great detritus of family, emerging
alone with a bloody knife, saying "I have cut
my way into the womb of the orphanage.
I am alone."

I am alone! The matrons had always
been alone, always. They could understand.
Orphans were proud — survivors
from another life killed off, a dozen lives.
They were thoroughbreds — pure —
born from vanished breeds.
Why hadn't the train killed them too?
Why hadn't the fire? The bush of tumors?
They were *magic*. Such survivors
received from the buxom matrons
hate akin to the strokes of love,
hate that went in and out, hate that warmed.

But the children of living drunks
or women who ran off with truckdrivers

or locked their children out to eat mulberries
in the churchyard tree were marked as weak,
unworthy of love or hate, hardly worth
beating — they were not scarred over
like orphans, not hard as agates
though like orphans they had no surface
that could bear a kiss. They wept
more, they stared less.

Thus, while the orphans had ice cream
or were rocked to sleep
in the valleys of buxom matrons who had at last
relented, deciding to love only
the most needy cases, we stared at skyscrapers
where our mothers took their lovers down.
We wet our pillows with tears in the narrow
coffins of our bunk beds.
We vowed to kill orphans, whose gurgles
we heard down the hall as they enjoyed
their intolerable freedoms,
far past midnight, learning to laugh
like rats in alleys, learning to survive
as only the children of true spirits can,
whose mothers are stars,
whose fathers are ash,
whose cousins are the pebbles around rose
bushes which would not even tear
the nylons of false mothers as they fled us.

ENVOI
(For Marilyn)

And the journalist will say you lie
you didn't wear uniforms, you didn't suffer,
you weren't torn from your senile grandmother's arms
you weren't forced to lift your hand
even to wash ten thousand dishes.
You spooned no pond until it was empty
and no one, no one, ever touched you.
He will tell it like it was,
as if being there disqualified *you*
from telling us.
He was right, no one touched you — touch,
Marilyn, as you knew, is such a gentle thing.
So gentle you touch me even now
who never came into my room or lay your
life frail as a rose petal against my face.

HYMN TO AUNT EDRIS

That I did love thee . . . O, 'tis true! . . .
Why, I will see thee in Philippi then . . .
Now I have taken heart thou vanishest.
Ill spirit, I would hold more talk with thee . . .
        — Shakespeare, *Julius Caesar*

Old katydids in the West Tulsa night!
Refineries burning off their oil in fiery pools.
Uncle Henry holding a picket sign in wind that whipped him.
At night, on his shoulder, holding hair, I stooped
through the doorway of the soup kitchen
where we bent over a long table, eating soup,
a family of hundreds, and went back for more.
Tell me again where my father's supposed to be.
Aunt Edris, your great swinging breasts
were pendulum of time too I see now, but then
this small boy wished to press his cheeks
against you, and couldn't tell you,
and you were young, though I didn't know it
then, laughing that Henry's toes were cold.
Your bed sounded warm, through that curtain
that hung between us. On the floor
we children threw cockroaches from us,
the only ones who loved our bodies,
and heard your giggles, tickles, guessed
at your rolling movements, tried to ape them
on our own flat bodies. But you turned

into a dolphin in the night, swam
as we could not, bore Henry
through the tossing waves, then wept.
More whys and wherefores to puzzle us!
The smell of your biscuits woke us
and you put us on the ice-cold table while
we watched you move in flannel about those warped
linoleum floors. The oven had a handle
made of coiled and gleaming wires.
Only for you would I run those errands
through ditches to bring back butter
that was not butter, had no color;
and later Henry left the picket lines
and his face became something that we always
feared. He threatened to throw us off
the bridge. Fourth of July he threw
firecrackers at us, had the dog chase us
round and round the house, under clotheslines.
Unwanted. So be it. But you I still want.
And dear woman find in the face of my own beloved
whose face is round as a biscuit, like yours,
and smiling, for she won't mistreat me.
Take me again, Edris, out to the outhouse,
in the rain, stepping from plank to plank.
It's our house, of cracked and rotting wood.
The lightning shows your face up close.
You hold me in your arms, and step lightly,
shaking, avoiding spiders, and the years.

A MEMORY OF WEST TULSA AND LONG BEACH

My Uncle Henry
spent his last heroic days
on the long beach in Long Beach,
picking up trash,
condoms from the night before,
beer cans.
And his woman went more and more shrivelled
as they lived out their life
in the trailer park
where she cleaned the toilets
and changed the light bulbs,
she who'd been, I swear it,
more beautiful than Helen of Troy.
I still think of those hot nights
in West Tulsa
when he must have been the luckiest
man in the world
just to lie next to her,
hand cupping her breast
or stroking the hair she'd let down.
So far inland, and yet that was where
I first heard the heavy sighs of the sea
and the rolling joy of infinite possibility.

IN THE GALLERY ROOM

Love divides love. And so, my son,
You choose the happy *Dell*
By Constable, a wading cow,
Silvered tree, a stag, old footbridge
Where you want, you say, "to wade
And take a nap."
After a hundred years this scene
Is fine and cold
On your naked, Brancusian feet.
Your favorite painter, you say,
Is John Constable.
But I choose *Low Ebb*,
In dun and lead, with heavy
Heart choose that — where Gustave
Courbet shows folks in fog
Just barely making it,
The storm about to close
Upon them, making sea's mean
Waves and sky all one.
And that is what you save me from —
By saying there too
You'd like
"To wade and take a nap."

ON THE PHOTOGRAPH "YARN MILL" BY LEWIS W. HINE

(For Samuel Cyrus David Ray)

A boy, age about eleven,
looking just like my son Son —
same flaxen hair, same cap
I gave him — long-sleeve
shirt tucked in overalls,
standing between iron spinning
mules in a yarn mill, his dirty
right hand touching the machine,
which is huge and black like oil
and no doubt clacking away, stamped
"MASON MACHINE WORKS
PATENT MASS 1903" in a circle
around a nub, like the other,
so that he is caught between
those two great breasts of iron
that face us. His left hand
hangs free and we could reach
out and pull him safe. Spools
of yarn recede down rows
beyond him as in the mirrors
of a barbershop; the humming
strings look like the innards
of long pianos whose music dins;
the yarn is beaten now by wooden

mallets, then woven — sheared,
combed, dyed — whatever
the boss men say, in North Carolina,
1908. The boy's face, like Sam's,
is trusting, gazes almost amused
at what's before him. This year,
luckily, a horse. Not a yarn
mill. In a dream last night,
I watched my son assemble
the temple of his life as from
a kit (he was named for kings)
and now I see him standing
between those steel machines,
a boy who had no temple,
who could reach out and touch
that cold iron breast,
then knock it off to joke with men.

GARAGE SALE

We came for the old days.
Bride's portrait in her veil.
And from the rocking chair
she herself — same long nose —
waves aside objections:
"Take it and the marriage

license too!" As if there'd
been no light, no spindle
post, no moaning at the bar,
no silver dollar in
the oaken drawer. Upstairs
you'll find the gown, white lace
for which I'm game three bucks.
The years of wind and fog
and fallout breathing through
attic louvers have gilded
nothing; a groom is not
an heirloom and nothing's
not for sale, for a dime
or a dollar — here's grampa's
collar. *Communitas*
is here, and here, and here,
upstairs and down where our
busted armor sprawls with
five of six blue willow —
ware — such sharing's rare when
not in dreams or on Brook
Farm or lost Oneida.
Or are we out to praise
Das Kapital? (Some stuff
we give away, just ask.)
Yes, dreams . . . or world's bright end
when all are called upright
by a shined up trumpet
and strumming of the glued-

together dulcimer. The aunts
and cousins watch from deck
chairs placed upon double
drives and offer smiles and
glimpses of their chest moles.
And when we flee, across
a lawn, chipped Chippendale
and Ben's Big Little books,
beside some toilet propped
for sale, with graffiti
haiku on its tank, we
stumble on rich cousin
George's wrecked electric
train, forgotten fifty years.

THE FATHER

What I did was lead them up
into the bus,
past Mexican ladies, men
seeking jobs in different cities,
grandmothers with parcels
they wanted me to lift
onto the overhead rack.
The two of them settled

into their seats, by blued
windows, and I kissed them,
handed them money,
said "Don't forget,
Daddy loves you . . . "
and stood by the station door
swathed in exhaust fumes,
waving, sending another kiss
again and again, oblivious
as one is with lovers,
overcome. I was overcome
for days, wet about the eyes,
not hearing when spoken to.
Keeper of the mint,
engravings, portraits, signatures.

THE THEME OF MISSED OPPORTUNITIES

glows in the dark.
We are all in the room of
the mind together,
no matter how it didn't
get across,
how no one spoke, or reached out.
Now that it's too late

love comes home
like a lamb of your own
sacred spirit, still searching
in all this snow.
You find someone who seems
to know all about it,
who brings moonlight
into the room,
pours it on all those broken
flowers.

IN TORNADO COUNTRY

In tornado country
the nudists are sitting
under the trees.
Their children are splashing.
Their trailers and tents
are cheap and elegant
in the lower winds
off bean fields, creeks.
And in the storm
they'll bellow out,
hold their own
while the clapboard
of farmers blows

away with rusty nails.
And I would like
to join them, with you.
Their women create
an alive museum
with their olive bodies
and seem more eternal
than stone,
even when they leap
into the pool, or smile.

THANKS, ROBERT FROST

Do you have hope for the future?
Someone asked Robert Frost, toward the end.
Yes, and even for the past, he replied,
that it will turn out to have been all right
for what it was, something we can accept,
mistakes made by the selves we had to be,
not able to be, perhaps, what we wished,
or what looking back half the time it seems
we could so easily have been, or ought . . .
The future, yes, and even for the past,
that it will become something we can bear.
And I too, and my children, so I hope,

will recall as not too heavy the tug
of those albatrosses I sadly placed
upon their tender necks. Hope for the past,
yes, old Frost, your words provide that courage
and it brings strange peace that itself passes
into past, easier to bear because
you said it, rather casually, as snow
went on falling in Vermont years ago.

THE MATTER OF SOCIAL LIFE

When I think of the dead, the illustrious
ones that is, with their names ringed golden
round a diadem, as at Ravenna,
certain ones of their number, who have joined
the immense majority, where even Katherine Mansfield
lives, what strikes me as hardest of all to grasp
is that each of these, certain of their number,
took a few precious instants to know nothing
more significant than me, perhaps at Oscar's party
when we stood together, sherry or beer in our hands.
And Oscar himself chatted with me too,
with that tongue that parsed the famous poem
about the butcher shop, when he saw the beef's tongue
along with his riven ribs still bloody

in the window, the fat streaks like frozen clouds.
Immortal, wonderful lights! These lights have gone on
to join the other lights, as· on the brilliant string
of incredible wattage over the five acre lot of Cadillacs.
And then a second wonder hits and makes me feel
a pathos in my gut. Certain of the living will not budge
or bother speaking, will not waste a moment on me.
They seem so immensely cocksure, more sensible,
pragmatic, than the immortal dead, who spoke to me
before they spoke to Katherine Mansfield, Dante, Homer
(and found out if he was a dozen women . . .)
And yet they are not dead at all, these who waste
no time, who do not speak back when I greet them.
They merely·choose, with their time, to cut me dead.

SONNET TO SEABROOK

In New Hampshire's green paradise this June
one sees the slowly radiating scars
of what may become an Inferno soon,
and even demonstrators bring their cars.
An ugly crater's opened in the earth,
by those devil's toys, earth-scraper, -mover.
Men strangely take an insane pride, giving birth

to disaster, like a twisted lover.
Where are our Thoreaus and our Emersons?
Lying in their graves, not so deep as this!
The earth is hollowed, spooned in helpless tons.
Death is promised in slow doses, like bliss.
Technicians tell us Armageddon's fine.
Cranes hover over shale. Slow rivers shine.

THE CENOTE AT CHICHEN ITZA

Leaning upon that chalky cliff
you held your breath and wondered at
strange perfection of the walls, pure
circles cut by rain where moss hung
like dead hair, and great green cacti
straggled down the walls like spiders.
The deep and stagnant water, green
too, seemed to lure more than those stones
two clowning toughs threw in, standing
on the clay parapet the priests
had left, who wore sacred feathers
when they threw their best victims in.
Dark was coming fast that Friday
we saw it, this immense sink hole,
and felt something beneath the scum
wanting us, alluring where quartz

skulls, onyx knives, golden women
with their jewels fell and fell for
sixty feet, like birds unique and
special to their time as we, Dear,
are not to ours. You held on tight
and later said you almost jumped
out past the caverns pocking walls.
But tourists need not leap, I said,
nor be taken in by darkness.
That place of death looked exactly
like what it was. You held your breath
and screamed when that German threw in
lizards he'd caught on pyramids.

THREE FROM GREECE

1. *In the Courtyard*

The wine-dark sky:
Evening is here.
Who wants to go set the table
        me
           me
me   me   me

meee   meee   meee
ME
      ME
I get to   It is evening.

2. *Crete*

The little black octopus
dances
     with the happiness
of reunion
     on the side of
the repaired
     amphora.

3. *Seen from a Ship*

They were tired when they got there,
these stones collected
     from the sea, now
climbing the Cretan hills.
     Blue haze settles.
Stone upon stone, they crawled
     upon themselves
while grapes and hands
     grew thick between
and ships sailed round
     like this we're on

BASKIN'S WOODEN ANGEL

In Utica, a brewery town in grey,
we pass the tempting chance
to sip free beer, trudge through freezing slush
and find the local oasis for the arts,
leftover inside green from summer's fire,
and find your angel standing there,
a nude nebbisch of a man, middle-aged,
hacked out of light wood, ash perhaps,
and two great Miltonic wings upon his back,
twin arcs descending in parabolas of woe —
and my own shoulders are hurting
from an old affliction
which your fellow spirit standing helps me
understand. I see the weighty wings
are fitted on through slots
as if a man might lift and set them down
and be relieved —
though he could not himself reach
quite so far behind.
                          The weights we carry
help us seldom toward a flight,
and rarely make another offer love.
I see this man as still a member of
his family in the woods. Yes, best
to set the wings aside
and best of all, to join the woods again,

the trees that do not urge
themselves or others to be a man
or angel or work of art, to be admired
by gaping crowds who should
be nudging at each other to get help
in setting down those burdens on their backs.

THE FARM IN CALABRIA

Sometimes I feel
    we don't live on a farm
        but in a Breughel painting.
As I head down
    into the valley
        in the morning to get
Our first jug of water I see
    far below, distanced by
        terrace after terrace
The man digging potatoes
    the flash of his hoe
        the flesh of his hand
And here the ambition
    to be above all steam
        of corruption is
Declared even by wisps
    of smoke or cloud

           that play above
The grapes, held in the daring
        sun, floating far
               below my meandering
Path that dips zigzag
        below the chestnut
               tree. Childhood
Brought me here: this is
        the self-same farm
               though cousins
Are gone, and Pickett
        Prairie, those white
               fences, and the
Crossroads of a dusty Eden are no
        more to be found, where
               we hadn't
Stumbled into clods
        of radiation. Here
               I am again
Myself, my son who follows
        after, my Sam
               who's scared
Of pigs and wants
        to be above
               his fears. Here
I find again
        my childhood and for Sam
               it is a tatter

A scrap of life so
      vivid he will search
            again for when
We went down
      into the valley to find
            the spring, into
A valley we share
      in the minds of Germans
            who bivouacked here
Who left craters
      where the apples grow
            and green ammunition
Boxes in the barn.

II.

This country has a dreamy
      mist each night, when
            ghosts change watch
And people touch us
      with their gifts
            of wine and greens
And chestnut hearts.
      And afternoons old
            Adelina
Shells her peas
      upon the porch

                    and cuts some
Dandelion greens — dandy lions
        my son's favorite
            flower —
Half for her, half for us
        and she tells me all
                about her hero
Mussolini and how he
        helped the people.
                Many too
She says and fans her bosom
        die
                for every leader
Many must
        die
                for every leader
Many must
        die, *molti, molti,*
                molti, she begins
To weep for sons
        and for the German
                boys she fed black
Bread
        and then she stands, bends
                over, tipping
Her pail of peas
        wrapping clothesline
                cord around

Her ancient legs
          to show what the crowd
                    did to Mussolini
and his girl, two
          pigs she said, when they
                    were through, one
With the other. We have
          found the old farm
                    but all our Fascist
Cousins gone.

III.

We cannot get together
          with them Sundays
                    for picnics
And pictures that fade
          overnight or disappear,
                    in ships at sea.
No more with them, Eulys
          and W.T., do we lean
                    against the fence
With paper plates. We have
          drifted from the land
                    and found it
As it was, lost in the day's
          fine madness, a farm

              lost in fog,
Turned into an island
            and in the daylight
                  raised by shadows
As the postman rides
            up our yellow road
                  as if on a red
Dimestore motorcycle
            from the Thirties
                  or on some despatch
Rider's wheels out of World
            War I, avoiding
                  craters where
The apples flew, black apples flew.

NEW POEMS

VILLANELLE: THEIR ARRIVAL

I'd like to place bright flowers by their bed,
something that would say we thought much of them
when we went climbing where grey donkeys fed.

That mountain gave a clear view, as I said,
of the lake below and the way we came.
I'd like to place bright flowers by their bed.

I tiptoed toward red blossoms but a maid
watched me from a doorway till I was gone,
when we went climbing where grey donkeys fed.

Poinsettias provoked my red-flower greed
as if they were sexual or had gold on.
I'd like to place bright flowers by their bed.

I shopped along the walls where a busy trade
in peanuts and chiclets is carried on,
when we went climbing where grey donkeys fed.

Such flowers could say better than I said.
I'd like to make them feel they're really home.
I'd like to place bright flowers by their bed
to say we climbed as high as donkeys fed.

A PORTRAIT OF THE MEXICAN BARBER

A humble man, he stands
beside his chair,
his own hair needing trim.
He wears a plaid wool jacket for
his shop front has no door.
On a hook above the half-silvered
mirror, a talcum brush and clippers
touch his profiled head, Aztec
I think. He's got an oil can,
radio, and testament. The cup
and tiny pot are both for tea,
no tequila unless I read him wrong.
In Spanish we get through
how many years I have and children and
how I like the temperate *clima*
and how my father was a barber too.
The cold enamel chair he touches
with oxblood leather on its arms
is not the one
my father shoved against for years
and moved from town to town. Once it sat
high on a truck of junk, was splashed
with midnight rain while mother wept
in dashboard light and father drove.
The landlord chased us with a gun.
Nor am I still the boy of wounded eyes

who when the trade was slow
climbed up to sit on a crooked crate,
a mannikin for practice trims.
On father's wall a picture hung of
great Long Hair Custer, in blue shirt,
white collar stars, red strangling kerchief.
He made his last stand on his knees
with pistol raised while all around him
the yelping braves took scalps.
He'd come to murder, stayed to die.

THE WISE GUYS
"Nature knows neither kernel nor shell."
                                        — Goethe

They're so smart they can speak
to a single cell and make it squeak.
They play Bach
while they watch their rockets rise.
Their computers can whirl and solve
any problem, yet leave us free
to stand in mud and slug each other
bloody
not noticing the sky and mountains.
After the corn is down
they plan to sail round the seas

with some of the things they know.
Now what they know is that
electron microscopes
turn up Horsehead nebulae
or the streets of Heraklion
with smell of lamb.
also that the Marne's barbed wire
is found in the foxfire
of human brain.
And endless explosions in the skin
will go on crackling
when Masabi magnets
speak to seas, dancehalls
cleared and empty,
kernel and shell no more.

TRAVELLING AND SITTING STILL

You think you're going someplace
When you're sailing through the sky
At five miles up, over the Pacific.
Or when you're jammed in the station
Waiting for the train to Kyoto
Or when the streetcars are clanging
Or it's shove against shove to get a table
Where you eat *sushi* or something Hungarian,

When you're filling out forms or handing
The passport over or even waiting
For a bus next to a greasy pylon.
You're consumed in travel, in just
Getting through. You take care of
Yourself. Time takes care of itself.
The ship with lowered sail
Arrives to bear you back. Moon's out.
But there comes a moment, be it in Wales
Or deep in the hold of that ship plowing
Deadhead through the night.
That it's back again to the essential.
The cup of tea is here, not so elusive
As snow on Snowdon or Fuji.
So what's the use of Tokyo?
The work room's shared with a cricket
Or a flea, and the cup of tea, the napkin,
Light, and time that is taking care of itself.

THE TOURIST

rides through Belgium
spots a crater
but an apple tree grows therein,
nothing going on just now,

a cow or two
between shows.
So he argues with
the concierge.

KITTY RETURNS TO AUSCHWITZ

A woman returns to Auschwitz
telling her son
who strolls beside her —
"This is where I shat — "
row upon row upon row
of holes in iron planks.
"This is where the S.S.
herded all my friends
into a truck —
This is where I said farewell
to my sister —
This is where I buried
gold off the bodies — "
And she stoops and digs
till a necklace
turns up. "And this is where
the shot bodies fell
into the ditch — " She claws
and hands him a bone

which he, being a doctor,
identifies — a man's elbow.
"Perhaps it is your grandfather,"
she tells him and briefly
weeps, adding her tears
to the puddle which already
holds molecules of bodies,
her sister's, her mother's.
We look over her shoulder
at the captured photograph
album, visit the warehouses,
pyramids of hair,
mountains of coats passed on
to the cold men of Stalingrad.
Here, stripped in the snow,
threatened with guns,
are the naked robbed
of their coats. Once I knew
an old Jew who could whistle
the fourth Brandenburg through.
He was the kind
here herded like oxen.
And Kitty, who had
to return, listens by birches,
no Brandenburg there,
just wind of the great Nothing.
These days she swims,

rebirth her theme, stares
at the test tubes she holds up,
afraid of the worst.

ON THE ISLAND

Santa Eulalia was a good place to be
on the Day of the Dead. Air was clear,
sky blue. Boredom was a bit of a problem
for expatriates, but there was a walk well
worth taking round the edge of town,
down unpaved lanes past white adobe shacks,
casitas, where one *perro* after another came out
and barked, or quit lapping muddy water and looked up.
Naturally one continued on up the hill
where all the fancy tombs had plastic flowers
and several women wept, hiding their faces
in black wool shawls. And there were fancy crosses,
gilt and ribboned, imported from Barcelona
on the overnight boat we had taken ourselves,
getting very drunk and angry in the lounge.
Down below, the town glittered in the sun —
one could see forever — one's wife and kids
were somehow getting through their human day.
Even in Spain all that pre-school babble

was a chaos like untangling gum from hair.
A day arrives when one just gives up, sends
them off with briefcases stuffed with apples,
just as one gives up and returns to America.
At night in Santa Eulalia there was dancing and love
that one simply danced or strolled into —
for example, a major love of my life came
from just walking a lady downhill in sharp moonlight.
But in such a blue of morning one could not
see the black night, the drinking, the timelessness,
nor hear that Beatles song that was that year's favorite.
Nor would I wish on anyone the vision of the gulls
and tourist husbands Sunday morning pacing seawalls
till their beloveds reappeared like drifting seaweed.
In a little chapel all the Spaniards place
their favorite snapshots above the saints
and bless them, leaving ribbons off their ladies' hair.
The tiny candles whip and flame through day and night,
as bright as ever on the morning of the Day of the Dead,
when it was splendid not to be in Portland
where the rain was, or anywhere on a risky plane
or bored to death in some committee meeting.
The sea beyond the island lay complacent,
undinal, yes. But that was sunlight sparkling
in the distance, beyond the town, toward Carthage.

TO QUEEN ELIZABETH

Queen, it's very cold
in your park.
Your flag is flying,
high on that battlement.
I figure there's not much
chance of meeting you.
The ducks are nice
in water at my feet,
flown in from all over
your empire, some prize
paddlers from Canada,
ladies' hats
upon their backs.
Your willows weep.
I like my own
garden more, without
this traffic roar
and so very many faces
my voice could not
make friends with,
even if I spoke,
hailing them with stout
heart and sticking out
my hand to shake.
In this Serpentine
that flows

I hear a lady drowned
named Harriet, dumped
by Shelley. And there's
history in your greenhouse,
right? I'm cold,
cold, lonesome, broke. Somewhere
near the brink.
Got anything to drink
around here? Tell me,
Queen, just tell me if
you're serving tea today
in where it's warm
or what? Winter roses
through the fogged up panes,
nice, nice! And fog.

THROWING THE RACETRACK CATS AT SARATOGA

Such cats are useful to calm the horses,
to purr and move among their horny hooves.
In fact a cat will fit precisely there
under the fetlock, bandaged half the time.
Thus they're gathered up in arms, from alleys

of cities, and brought to Saratoga.
When some horse named Herod or Whiskers wins
some low and humble cat has done his share.
But then great vans are backed against the stalls:
It's time to wend down South, to Long Island

or Kentucky. In long trailers for nine
horses we find no feline room at all.
Hence this ritual called the thowing of cats.
Both black and white men stand and toss them high,
cats of every color, every lineage.

Over the fence of steel they sail, claws spread.
They brush the pines and land beneath a bough.
Each looks about then like old Balboa,
finding himself quite lost, with dark coming.
His way is blocked back to his friend the horse.

These exiled cats do not confer; but start
in silence padding through the rustling leaves.
Behind them, sailing in parabolas,
their brothers fly like mewling cannonballs
or Roman candles spewing on the Fourth.

To die because you are no more of use
may also happen to a groom who throws.
But now he chooses not to think of that.
He merely finds a choice one, throws him high,

lofting toward a pine or the moon he spots

emerging like a silver dollar bright
and clean. First the cats and then the hosing
of stalls, the boarding up of all the doors,
that dull long trip to town, to one Skid Row
or another, where next year's alley cats,

pale kittens, stalk the legs of drunks for love.
As for these stumblers through the shadowed trees,
I've chosen one who lifts his paw just like
a horse he looks about to find, as I
absurdly seek and trust to find you still.

THE SNAKE PEOPLE

The dried skins make belts and hatbands.
The living snakes are wrapped around their arms
or dangled in the air. It's a mark of status
to have been bitten, and more survive
than statistics say they should — there's something
in religion that keeps a man's pecker up.
And by the way, they stroke them just as if
that's what they are, holding a rattlesnake
or cottonmouth — you'd swear it stuck

right through the fly. These rituals go
straight back to Greece, the mysteries and orgies.
Today they throw them back and forth.
The brave ones stand with rolled up sleeves.
The deacon bends to take them from a box
marked JESUS on the lid's inside
as if those snakes could read and be calmed
by such a word, a kind of snake mantra.
One thing it's important to remember is
the snake is just a symbol of the devil
who curled himself around an Edenic tree
then offered down a golden apple,
a snake who had a female head and tresses
as you can see in your highbrow *Book of Hours*.
It's all the same tradition. These Kentucky cultists
are pleasant if you get to know them.
They just don't want you saying things against them.
At times the snakes thrown back and forth real fast
seem a kind of stitchery, each twist and turn a knot
until the circle's bound together, tight
and glowing with a thin veneer of fear.

THE CIGARETTE FACTORY

Falling into the counting machine
by the millions they swarm, push

one another aside like furious
larvae, alive molecules
of living plants, viruses,
d.d.t., fallout, soon to enter
animals, to set their tissue
flaming, the cancer
that grew out of slavery,
that still glows in the millionaire's
eyes, out of the portrait staring
down at the beautiful black girl
who gives us a tour so proudly
saying "We own so much
all over the world, look
at the map," the bright pins
of a bold campaign, like
Rommel's, the foreign brands
translated like novels.
And our camel there has real
tobacco for hair, shaggy
and cute — stroke him on
your way out (our kids did).
Fashionable death —
therefore unfashionable to jeer
at it, or show concern!
Trivial death —
therefore trivial to speak of it!
Trite, acceptable death —
therefore out of line

to write a poem about it!
Enjoy the cool, unrippled pools
the millionaire provides!
Later we strolled his vast estate,
found little there he could not have had
without the trade in coffin nails,
a rustic shelter near his tennis courts,
an extra pond or two, and butterflies.

TENNESSEE

He lusts to walk around the town,
another urge they wouldn't understand —
They'll hail him from their cars
as if there's danger, force him
to ride round like a gangster, keep
his head down low and mutter answers
while the morning's golden air is locked outside
with leaves that seem to know
the very hour, even day, to die,
great rush downwards toward the dark.
He'd like to wade
but there's no pool left,
nor courthouse grass permissible for strolling,
and he has no key to wander through

the labyrinth that's on the way
to the official tarmac oval track.
And so he stretches inwardly
and gets to know the town as if
he too has something to remember.
On the corner stands, or leans upon a meter,
the old guy who greets all comers as if
returned from war. They surely
grew up here, else why would they return,
why gaze so blankly
at gold glitter built into the sidewalk
like a map of nebulae or birthday candles.
The used cars lift ten thousand pennants
toward the sky. They flutter
like a dancer's skirts. Charm too is on
the parking lot where some religious sect
in a circle flounces, sways, and jigs.
They're meant to bring the business in, but
their music brings a tear
as if they're dead brought back. A cousin
seems to wail and whoop in calico,
flung back half far enough to break her back.
The pallid sun through clouds of haze
by late day finds the poet tired
of travelling to and fro and within
this town where he's put up an extra day
and will take nothing with him,
not one memory of woman lent and leaning

toward the moon nor yet
a trinket from their dimestore offers
although he's lifted up a little cedar chest
quite clearly painted *Tennessee* in black
upon or under varnish. He's smiled and had
a word or two with more than one
who seemed to think inside a friendly bar
(the tender talked) that quite frankly
he really ought to stay — they deemed
him worthy of their comradeship. And yet
he's wise enough to know
that if he lingered, under lithographs of Lee,
they'd soon discover how
he's not the kind they *really* keep around.
The locked up lonely heart must make
its own way to the bitter end,
as if forbidden to find a single state
to stay in, but doomed to wander all,
to seek that friend whom casual others
idly mention, the one just left or about
to enter, a friend for life,
quite easily acquired or grieflessly forsworn,
replaced or turned up often
or mentioned in the postcards
worth far too much to auction.
For one pure moment the poet let a true friend

polish up a square of walnut bar.
It was a friend indeed who asked
about the leather elbows lifted, sewn on tweed.

MIGRANT MOTHER, 1936

She was drawn as if by "instinct,
not reason," had seen the sign,
PEA PICKERS CAMP, had driven on,
the road slick, but something
called her back. She had
to turn around, to find the woman
sitting on a box, huddled
in a tarp as if waiting
always for Dorothea Lange.
"I drove into that wet and soggy
camp and parked my car
like a homing pigeon." She asked
no questions, moved in silence
with the lens. The woman told her
she was thirty-two, had come
from the Dust Bowl. She and the children
had been living on frozen vegetables
from the field and wild birds
caught with hands. They had sold
all that would buy food, their tires,

did not know if they could ever leave.
She nursed the baby at her breast,
revealed the madonna, lover, mother,
pale half-moon pressed against the head.
The hungry lens looked equally upon
the lantern, tin pie-pan, hacked pole
that held the half-tent up.
The dirty baby lay as if he'd drunk
the milk of death. The older two
leaned sadly on their mother,
their clothing made of gunnysacks
or else the linen of Christ's shroud.
Dorothea took no names, and said no thanks,
nor handed bread across,
nor joked until those ancient children laughed.
But she put her ten eternal minutes in
and called it work, before the dark rain fell.

MARKS ON A WALL

You've drawn a frame
around these pencil marks,
their heights from your thigh
up to above your head now,
like lines on a tide-gauge.
You touch these marks,

and for some reason you feel
betrayed, angry at
these innocent creatures,
the one who at four
looked like a Bronzino portrait,
the girl whom you pushed
in a cardboard box
while she laughed and called
Choo-choo. You are not
a gracious loser. These dates,
though you scrawled them,
look like those on archaic
coins, found deep in the earth.
Those afternoons of sunshine
and pollen betrayed you.
You stood like a slave
minting such coins, scratching
the dates and the faces,
the angelic ones like emperors
who now stand tall in the distance,
seamarks like hillside stone
or persistent towers.
It is as if you'd have wished them
to arrest their own growth,
to refuse at all costs to leave
you by this wall that survives.
You chew this cud of remorse
like a vendor of starfish

who sprayed his catch
with plastic at just, he thought,
the right moment, offered
them for sale. Surely
it is your saintly, magnanimous
Buddha's integrity, paunchy,
good-willed, that kept you
from doing exactly that,
that helps you briefly
to forgive their going,
to understand they had
a rendezvous with destiny.

STAYING OVER WITH AUNT RUTH

She put the slices out
on her heirloom brocade chair
which has vanished with the years.
"Don't let the bedbugs bite,"
she said. "But first you can have
an orange, as sweet as candy."
She laid aside the peels
like people she discussed,
and rolled her stockings down.
Her man had been so mean
she had to tell us far

into the night, across
the flaccid light. He died
in a Skid Row fire but we recalled
how he hid our candy in his hat
and we climbed up on his belt.
No way she could slander him,
not when faces in the fire
had burned so bronze before.
She loved. He loved. We loved.
"Then let him have his whiskey,"
her sister said — she'd beg for love.
But he confirmed her tight-lipped
edict — death and winter chill
unto all drunks — my Uncle Mac as well.
They said the walls in that hotel
were made of chicken wire
and men were curled like scorched
tamales in their blankets.
Outside Aunt Ruth's back window,
mornings, we could see great balloons
afloat, long-nosed fish
above the alley cats, and bums
who rummaged through the barrels.
"If they're mean, just call me,"
she said, and took us back
to where no phone linked bedrooms up
with love. Sometimes at night
I recall the brand names of

her powder and perfume, the dimestore
stuff that gets put on with brushes and
with puffs. And her tiny, foolish shoes —
size two or three — she'd buy them off
a mannikin or doll. And her beads of shell.

FOR THE STEPFATHER

His grave has a rusty anvil on it,
I kneel there in soggy grass
recalling his huge flat hand
pressing the girl's waist
while she in innocence looked out,
wanting rescue, but also titillated,
not quite knowing what
it was all about. He'd called her
to his knees, she'd nuzzled up
against his beerbelly. He'd tickled
her, she him. She asked
why he use tobacco snuff, teased, and Lee
avoided the mother's puling need
for all his love, his great flat hands
that lifted anvils once.
And still I love their eyes,
their improbable near-coupling, the girl's

freckles which buzz like bees
upon her arms. And the musty smell
of the tavern, which seems to rise up
into my knees, out of this damp earth.
I recall Lee brooding in a booth,
his head between pale buttresses of hands,
mumbling, I think, to God, to be forgiven.
He knew it was not right, could never be,
tiptoing toward the bathing girl
until she rose up tall in the circle of
that galvanized tub of tin.
Lee, great awkward plowman who stood
and gazed until the thin girl screamed,
I forgive this ravage of my sister
and wish I could forgive for her.
And weep belated tears
upon your rusty anvil, for all
                                    old stumbling men.

ANOTHER GARAGE SALE

All she had was a giant wooden salad fork
hanging on a wire fence.
All she had was a box of *Rolling Stones*
bleached out in the sun.
All she has was a bunch of potted

house plants she'd decided
not to take along in her rusted-out Datsun.
All she had was a marriage manual
thumbed with the spine busted and a coffee
or vaseline stain on the cover
a stain round and wobbly and tobacco colored.
All she had was
big bruises on her legs, a hard
woman to love (I realized as she stood
above me with pale legs in green
jogging shorts with the number 6
on the right thigh and a movie usher's
ribbon on the side). All she had
was love maybe. In any case all she had
was brown hair scrubby as a fox's
shoved aside to show
glistening eyebrows like Madras rain
sweat on her brow, a mystic smile
at her lips, ready for about anything
I'd say as I squatted looking at the issue
of *Rolling Stones* documenting what a drunk
Charles Bukowski is. All she had
was freckles like pansies in a field,
the sweatshirt crossing them and blotting
out the best. All she had was dazed eyes
that said all but love for sale. And maybe that.
All she had was bitter lips, squint eyes
that said Damn It's Hot and all she had

was the mystery of what she'd do inside
or who she'd meet
back in her shadowed air-conditioned room again
that hung above the drive like a box seat
over the flat stage of the tarmac drive
where her Garage Sale was playing. According
to the critics it was the saddest
sorriest most shadeless and disreputable
garage sale in town. On the way back
to my own sidewalk I saw her front
curbside trashpile where she had thrown
out better things than those for sale.
There she'd tossed her great red bolster
cushions, her lacy lamp and other
props of joy and sin, leftovers from
her little private brothel or so
I chose to think on my way to lunch.

THE OLD MAN WITH THE SHOPPING CART,

wire, stolen from Milgrim's, is dead.
I used to see him at one garage sale
after another, filling up his cart
with what he'd bargained for or walking
down the street tugging it

or turning back to tell some kid
how to haul his goods. He looked
like some survivor of Rommel's Afrika
Korps, just got fat, bald, grey,
told me once he was retired, on optometrist.
One summer evening when the sky
was rosy he hailed us walking by
and gave us five overseeded sumac trees,
the midget velvet fronds that grew
like rhubarb all over his yard —
now they're our great staghorns —
but his yard is full of trash, black
plastic bags full of dynamoes and junk,
and inside there's even more.
We go in, ducking the narrow door,
and find ourselves amazed.
What a champion packrat he really was!
Everywhere boxes, stacks of surplus
this and that, sheets, tablecloths,
sails not unfurled. A Jello box
of magazines, those pink
and showered bodies, that pulchritude
and stuff of harems, shoved in tight,
and portraits in their oval frames.
He must not have passed up, ever,
anything. The crowd is plodding through.
A lady lifts a tied-up bundle, five hammers.
Shovels line the wall. And in the back

is that room of scattered lenses
like monocles of ancient uncles.
The archaic eye chart curls upon the wall.
A wire chair leans as if caught
in dusty air, half turned over.
The room is like Miss Haversham's.
All's here except her cake. You find
a meter that measures light
and we buy it though the case is cracked.
Outside we hold it up, hope
it's not too late to catch some luminescence.
The man's in his khaki shorts
standing in Charon's boat, directing
how to row, and not to tip, not spill
his tied-up papers, dolls, glass jars,
rusty wagon missing wheels. He peers ahead.
At that dark tunnel's end
it's almost blinding, all the light
he was peering toward, prowling streets
to find, haggling after. His hands splay
out to reach it, and he almost tips
that boat, but Charon helps him, helps.

THE ESKIMO GIRL

In Alaska an Eskimo girl
dances in a sod house,
raises her arms
as if to dance,
to show for the photograph
that she could be lifting
herself upward like flame,
happy as a courtesan.
But in the small room
of this dirt hut
her red skirt means nothing
blazing beside pain.
Hers is the honor
not of dancing
for the emperor, but of having
more radioactivity
in her blood
than any other American.
For this she has been sought
out, honored
because she ate the caribou
that stared at the horizon,
caribou which had eaten
lichen, green over the iced
rocks, lichen which had
innocently lifted into itself

the fallout of our bombs,
the magical cesium
and strontium and blue cobalt.
In a still photograph
she looks like a Thai dancer
with arms thrown out.
She looks as if she is about
to burst into flame.
Her blood is cold now,
cold by now,
it ages well on the permafrost,
it ages like the blood
of seals and caribou.
It marks the porcelain plate
of Napoleon.
But the old emperors would have let
her live, would merely have made her
one of their whores, and let her dance.

ANOTHER ASSASSIN: NEGATIVE CAPABILITY

"I have two luxuries to brood over in my walks, your loveliness and the hour of my death. O that I could have possession of them both in the same minute. Your's ever, fair Star . . . "
— Keats to Fanny

"The horror is that there is no horror."
— Kuprin, *Yama*

The assassin ate his eggs
and was rude to the waitress.
In the hotel room
he was bored
and the maid later said
there was nothing special
to report — he'd looked bored,
that's all, when she entered.
The only suspicious thing
she'd noticed was . . . the T.V.
was off, not on —
he wasn't watching daytime soaps.
He'd ridden buses three days
from L.A., leaned
against a post in the Greyhound
station across from the White
House. He had not
gone to Ford's theatre
or any porn movies
or live shows; no prostitutes
recognized his picture
or recalled any particular

propositions.
Those throughout the land
who had read radical
anarchism into his act
or Nazi sentiments or
a penchant for
the dialectical·thing to do
or a thirst for fame
were proved —
when the facts came out —
all wrong. He was, it seems,
just trying to please
an actress he had seen
in a very violent film
and guns were cheap
and required no particular
demonstration of sanity.
It was a cheeseburger
he ate, in the Greyhound
terminal cafe.
But I made it eggs
because I always like to change
something, in my pursuit of
Negative Capability, and her Bright Star.

RIBCAGE BEHIND A MEAT COUNTER

I glance in admiration
at this, left handiwork,
abandoned shell. In last
thin detail
his excellence adheres. It's been
a cold year and a busy, rib
bones brought seldom
to full expansion, broad
like that one emptied, aery,
Crystal Palace-grand; liver
often taxed; oysters sluggish;
blood fatigued. I know
they drove him through a ditch
with sticks. I know
they hurt him with more
than gross and major
death, with all the little
social ones. Made him eat
iron, saw
no goodness in him
or his bones. Yet here
like latticework, well-
spaced arcade, shadow-making,
alabaster crouching, his action
is not yet final and
the butcher hacks elsewhere.

SAINT FLANNERY

"She could never be a saint, but she thought she could be a martyr if they killed her quick."

— Flannery O'Connor

At Lourdes everybody drank from the cup
passed around. She put her metal crutches down
and counted those ahead — about forty.
In Rome she sat eager on the front row
and the Pope gave her a special blessing
"on acct. the crutches." She felt herself
a twelve year old, "a very ancient twelve,"
yet watched him as she would her characters.
He had "the special super-aliveness
that holiness is." She'd seen it in swans,
peacocks, Muscovy ducks and Chinese geese.
Now she who said she'd see us all in hell
before she made her first graceful move must
accept these candles brought on knees to her.

THE TELEPHONE

One evening we sat in perfect silence
By the telephone when a strange event occurred —
And I heard one by one the old voices
As if they came to the center stage, each
To have his say. First came the slanderers,

A few who said they'd meant for twenty years
To tell me how intense had grown their hate,
Their envious anger. And they were glad
When I told them I had suffered, they had
No need to envy anything. And then
My late father spoke — confession most strange —
He'd after all had regrets, had not been
The brute he'd always seemed, especially
With his silences that endured for years.
And there were the women, in whom despite
Myself I'd kindled love. By convention
They had curled round into themselves like scrolls,
Archaic texts that still need translating.
One confessed self-love, my name on her lips.
And Mother called, to say that she was ill,
And Daughter, to hint for some green Spring cash,
A needed trip to the Virgin Islands,
And she says she's tired of modelling nude,
Still has an urge for earthquakes, Santa Cruz,
and her dead lover Steve, whose Dad she wants
To visit soon. A host of others called
To say they cared and some who wondered if
We would in this life ever meet again,
And at last I looked to the one who shared
The room with me and asked if she would speak,
But she was silent like a bronze penny.

GETTING TO KNOW YOU

"And now for a confession. I have a love of confession. I do not remember the face of my own father. My wife is in the next room as I sit writing, but I do not remember what she looks like."
— Sherwood Anderson, *Tar*

This weekend let's get
to know each other.
I have a love of confessions,
so I'll confess first.
That may help you
to get to know me.
If you reflect this awareness, my growing
self-awareness, I might see
what sort of fellow I am,
autumnal and rare and disappointing.
And you, tell me something too,
now that I am remembering
that your eyes are brown
and round like those mirrors
on the wall in Vermeer's painting
where the man has his hand
on the bride's warm globe of a pregnant belly.
And this something you hint of to me —
was animal . . . vegetable . . . mineral . . .
and happened years ago? Hearing helps
me truly know you, recall at least
your name. We've become so obscure
to each other, being so close.
We need to find

new entertainments, stroll through
the flea markets. I may find at last
a Harris tweed left by a dead father,
or a fine copy of a high school Latin text —
I may yet fulfill that old ambition
and she'll see it from the grave —
Miss Butts, O competent and Lesbian
teacher of Latin! I am her best boy yet,
though I knew not one conjugation.
On my knees I implore you to teach me,
to find your life's fulfillment —
wake me to the joys of Vergil and all
the minor makers of odes and epigrams.
Miss Butts broke chalk in her anger,
glared at us through lenses thick
as bomb sights. If there is a great sorrow,
get into it, says the mystic. It should be
a great relief — knowing the worst
is over, has long been over.
There are only these stray ends now,
of confession and reunion.

DE MORTUIS

I saw the dead with the skin
        off their faces
so that their eyes could not rest.
           Their hands
knew no idleness
though they lay in gloves
        of iron given
by their medieval friends.
Grandfather pulled me close
to tell me the lessons
        he had learned
reading the dirt for a lifetime
        with a scholar's
intent, not the ignorance
        of just any man
with a hoe. Watch the earth,
he told me, not puffed up
words of men, not women
        with ice in their teeth.
Then he sent me back
as if to our old shack of a house,
for a bucket of water,
a dipper he could lift in the sun.